So Long Joey

The Dave Boyer Story

with
Sonny Schwartz and Fred J. Hamilton

FLEMING H. REVELL COMPANY
OLD TAPPAN, NEW JERSEY

Scripture quotations in this book are from the *King James Version of the Bible.*

Grateful acknowledgment is given for use of the hymn "No One Ever Cared for Me Like Jesus" by C.F. Weigle. Words and Music Copyright The Rodeheaver Co., Owner. Used by Permission.

Foreword

God has really used you to change lives and we kids pray for you all the time . . .

Dear Mr. Boyer:

On the Tuesday morning of March 25, I woke up in the lowest state of mind I've ever experienced. Standing alone gazing dejectedly out the window at the gray morning, I suddenly burst into tears and sobbed uncontrollably. Why was the Lord doing this to me? I had no reason to go on living, and I wished with all my heart that there was some way I could quietly step out of life without hurting or affecting anyone else, and end my problems. But this was impossible for I'd hurt too many people that looked up to me and depended on me. Thinking then that my misery and suffering would only go on shook me more and more with unsuppressed sobs.

The past year had been the hardest in my life. Never before had I put so much in to my studies, struggled so hard with them, and gained so little. Every week I flunked my chemistry quizzes, several of which I couldn't answer a single question on. My grades were barely passing.

The greatest problem tearing at my life, however, was a physical problem that doctors haven't yet solved—something that seemed to hinder anything I might want to do and keep me from stepping out in the world on my own. I have a mild form of epilepsy which affects me at periodical intervals of about six weeks. I could write papers describing these spells, but I'll just tell how they leave me when they've passed. My mind is like a blackboard full of valuable information that has been erased. This material now needs to be collected again, organized, and rewritten. To a college student struggling frantically to write all she can on the blackboard of her mind, what is a greater discouragement than having it all erased and having to learn it over?

But my greatest heartache was the thought of how useless I was to God. Outside of serving Him and glorifying Him I had no reason or purpose for living. And it seemed I had no power to fulfill this purpose. How I managed to get to my first classes I don't know.

The Lord took my mind off myself and my problems that morning and turned my thoughts to Himself. As Dave Boyer sang "Oh, How I Love Jesus," the reality of those words became clear in mind as I heard someone singing words they truly meant. Here was a man who'd experienced much of the world and its heartaches—one who could realize how very much the Lord had done for him and learn to love the Lord with all his heart.

Well, the main purpose of this letter was to let you know how the Lord had used your testimony in the life of a young college student. My prayers are with you that the Lord will continue using you to reach others for Him—especially young people.

In Christ,

Virginia R.,
Los Angeles, Ca.

Dear Dave:

I just returned from the Ocean City (N.J.) Convention and I would like to thank you in a personal way for the blessing you have been to me.

I want you to know that my life has been changed since Ocean City this year.

Before coming to Ocean City I was living for R.A.G., (that's me) and no one else really mattered. I was always finding fault with the other guy when it was me that was really wrong. I picked on my little brothers so much that they hated me. And I let every little thing they did bug me.

On Thursday night when you gave your great testimony, which I have heard so many times before, it had new meaning and God really spoke to me. So I went home (to our travel trailer) and sat on my bunk and prayed and read God's Word. I asked God to take full control of my life, to take away this awful selfish way that was ruling me and guess what, He did it!

Now, I am almost a new person. I mean I look the same (unfortunately) except I smile a lot more but my actions have sure changed, praise God. I've started to think of the other guy a little bit. I don't bug my brothers so much. I'm so happy I want to share this abundant life with everyone.

                                        In His Love,

                                        Ruthie G.
                                        Lake Bluff, Ill.

Dear Dave,

I hope you don't mind my writing to you, but I had to let you know how God has been using you because when I first heard you sing, I understood the joy of being a Christian. I haven't told you this before, but before that time I almost committed suicide. I don't know exactly why, but it wasn't because I was bored or tired of living. But now I wouldn't even consider suicide because I have so much purpose.

So just thanks a lot for coming to Chicago, but even more, thanks to God. God has really used you to change lives and we kids pray for you all the time. Now it's my turn to say "God Bless you."

Love,

S.D.
Homewood, Illinois

Mr. Boyer:

I know that you don't know me, nor do I know you, but I pray that you read this letter.

I attended the Saturday evening service at Red Rock, Pa., on July 19, 1969. Through Christ in you I was touched by the Holy Spirit to stand forth and accept Christ and yet I still resisted. Is it too late to accept Him? Please pray for me, that at God's will He will touch me again and I will accept His call. I purchased one of your records and every time I listen to it I receive a blessing. Thank you for accepting Christ and witnessing in this fashion. Please pray for me.

Sincerely,

Josephine W.
Kingston, Pa.

Dear Dave:

I just can't begin to tell you how grateful both Nancy and I are to you. It means so much to me. I can't express the great feeling in my heart. It's sorta' a warm, glowing, happy, joyful, feeling. All of these words don't even come close.

I tried to tell myself I was saved, but now I know it was impossible to even think this. It was your sermon that did it. I've never listened as closely before tonight. I bet it was because you made it so interesting. With entertainment in it, it's so much greater. I really owe all of my thanks to you.

A friend always, love,

K.D.
Montrose, Pa.

(These letters speak for themselves. They tell of Dave Boyer's powerful witness to young people throughout the country—in towns, hamlets, and large cities. Dave Boyer's story touched their hearts, and it will touch yours.)

THE PUBLISHERS

Introduction

MY NAME WAS ONCE DAVE BOYER.

Then it was Joey Stevens.

Now it's Dave Boyer again.

This is the story of my life—first as the son of a revered clergyman, then as a successful nightclub entertainer, then as a boozed-up failure in life who depended on alcohol and narcotics to keep him going.

As a matter of fact I came within inches of taking my own life —but I found the Lord and was saved.

Now, I'd like to tell you about how I found Christ and my new life in Him.

So Long Joey

1

From Baltimore to Chicago, the Boyers carried the message of Christ in song and word.

We were a happy Christian family, dedicated to my father's ministry and the service of Christ.

JOEY STEVENS should never really have existed in the first place —not when you consider the family into which he was born. But you have to picture the family together as we were when I was a kid to know what I mean.

My father, the Rev. Ralph Boyer, was a man of great faith who founded the York Gospel Center in York, Pennsylvania, and who won the respect of such notable men of Christ as Billy Graham.

My mother, Anna Boyer, was born and raised in Philadelphia. Her father, a reformed alcoholic, found the Lord when she was about sixteen. My mother met my father while she was singing in various churches where he preached. She has a real God-given musical ability, and even as a young person was a musical leader. However, Anna Boyer was a wife and mother first, and even in very lean times she always made sure we ate well and made a nice appearance—on a preacher's small income, too.

I'm the youngest of six children—four brothers and two sisters. My oldest sister, Betty, is married to the Rev. William Pinkernell, whom God led into social work in Pennsylvania, studying for his master's degree. Until about a year ago, he was a preacher in the First Covenant Church, Rockford, Illinois.

Next in line is my brother Eugene, who led Joey Stevens to Christ. Eugene took over the York Gospel Center when my father died in 1965. Prior to that time he had been a missionary to France, and has since returned to that country where he heads the European Evangelistic Crusade. He recently introduced Gils Bernard, one of France's outstanding entertainers, to Christ. Gene and his wife, Charlotte, have two daughters, Carol Ann and Libby.

Following Eugene in age is Daniel, an insurance man in Minneapolis. A very active layman in the church, Daniel sings and is a fine musician. He and Lou have two girls, Becky and Sherry.

Then comes my sister Nancy who lives in Camp Hill, Pennsylvania. She, like my brother Daniel, is extremely active in church work. Nancy and her husband, Herb Fenstermacher, and their three children, Peter, Robin, and Shawn, belong to the Assembly of God Church in Harrisburg.

My youngest brother, and the second youngest member of the family is my brother Gerald, who has a marvelous tenor voice, is a choir director, an organist, a pianist, and my voice coach. He is also coproducer with my brother Eugene of a broadcast called "The Voice of the Gospel," which is distributed across the French-speaking world by an organization known as Back to the Bible, Inc. of Lincoln, Nebraska. Gerry and Ellie are parents of a son, Maurice Christian.

So that's the family. Now picture this:

There we are, my mother and father and six kids, piled into a Model-T Ford, heading out of Baltimore for York, Pennsylvania, where my father had established a small ministry.

It's the late 1930s, and the Boyer family, a musical family, a strong Christian family, an evangelistic family, is on the road heading to a church service to sing and pray and win hearts for Christ. This is a talented family, each in his or her own right a good musician and singer.

Eugene is a bass, my sister Betty a soprano, Nancy a marvelous pianist and soprano, my brother Daniel a beautiful baritone and trombone player, Gerald an organist and tenor, and me, a boy soprano. My mother sang and played piano, and my father would lead the family group and preach.

We would also break down into smaller groups—a girls' trio with my mother and two sisters; a boys' quartet, a boys' duet, or a solo.

The Boyer family was carrying the message of Christ in song and word. We were doing hour and a half programs in cities and towns throughout Pennsylvania, Maryland, and even as far away as Chicago. Hundreds—literally hundreds of people were finding Christ through these services. We were a happy Christian family, dedicated to my father's ministry and the service of Christ.

The family actually had its beginning in Baltimore, where I was born in 1934. Dad was with the United Brethern Church then and had established his ministry there. But in 1936, he broke away from the United Bretherns. The ministerial association had been expressing displeasure at his preaching the prophecies which were so much a part of his sermons. But Dad maintained he had to preach what God wanted him to preach, so it became a matter of principle. Finally, he decided to follow his conscience and brought his family to York in that Model-T Ford that was to become our mode of travel over the next few years.

To say the least, we had humble beginnings in York! The first week there, Dad held a Sunday school meeting in a church at the Negro armory. Only twenty-two people attended that first service, but Dad was as happy as if it had been 500. He knew he could make a go of it.

And his perseverance and hard work quickly paid off. Within four years he built the York Gospel Center—a church that could accommodate 1,000 persons. And he began bringing in a number

of well-known evangelists as special guests—men like Percy Craw-
ford and Billy Graham. I really do think one of the contributing
factors in helping that congregation grow so rapidly was our family
singing. The people in York loved it, and this was as much a tribute
to my father's leadership and guidance as it was to our talent. He
kept us together and united people around him. Of course, he had
the tremendous assistance of a loving and dedicated wife—my
mother—who directed all our musical efforts.

My father's greatest characteristic was his ability to communi-
cate the love of Christ to people. He was an innovator in his day.
To use the word *promote* would bring the wrong connotation to
the service of Christ, but Dad wasn't afraid to use a method.
Today, of course, men like Oral Roberts bring out Lou Rawls, the
jazz singer; Billy Graham's team has tremendous promotion men,
and Rex Humbard makes use of television media. The idea is to
get the message across—and that's what my father did.

But it was more than just reaching the people through a media
or a method, though. My father generated a special kind of love.
For example, I remember we were walking down a street in York
one day (me a little kid of four holding my father's hand). Suddenly
he pointed across the street and said to me, "Do you see that man
over there?"

"Yes," I replied.

"Well," my father said, "he doesn't like me. He hears me on the
radio and he hates everything I say, but I'm going over there and
say hello to him."

And Dad, still holding my hand, crossed the street, walked right
up to that man, and shook his hand!

Later he told me, "Jesus said we have to love our enemies.
Maybe I made a friend of that man today."

Dad also believed very strongly in his own prophecies. And the
way they are holding true so many years after they were made is

absolutely fantastic. This is best illustrated by quoting from one of his sermons which was delivered more than thirty years ago. Titled "The Four Watches of the Night," the sermon was printed and distributed to thousands of persons throughout the country. Here are portions of it and remember it was written more than three decades ago!

We are now in the fourth watch. The fourth watch of the night has come. Darkness and coldness increase constantly.

Many believed the World War would end war. Prophetic students declared this untrue. Humanity has learned that war is not over. With the close of the war came such a breaking loose of sin, immorality, crime and vice as the world had never seen before in one generation. Churches that were one time on fire for God, became cold and lifeless. Modernism came into the pulpit and worldliness came to the pew. Apostasy became outspoken in the Church and continues to increase in intensity.

While the world needs Christ as never before, modernistic critics argue as to whether He is true or not. Theological arguments have made Christendom the laughing stock of demons while countless millions have continued to plunge into Christless graves. What a picture! Darkness! Coldness! The Dawn must be near!

Immorality or Beastism receives the approval of society in most instances. Evolution in the schools is promoting animalism in society. I believe the Dawn is near, because the night is so cold and dark. Remember, the darkest and coldest period of the night is just before Dawn. Jesus is just around the corner. I am told that others were mistaken. "Don't you think you may be mistaken?" I'm asked. If others had studied the whole Bible they would not have sold all and gone to housetops, wearing pillowcases, etc., waiting for Christ to come.

Jesus said, "Occupy till I come." I have frequently pointed out that certain outstanding events appear in the Bible that will be fulfilled in the end time of the age, preceding the Second Coming of Christ.

Here they are, briefly stated:

Federation of Western Nations
Two great irreconcilable Ideologies
Great North-Eastern Confederacy
Israel restored as a nation
Struggle for commerce
Movement to World Government
Movement for Ecclesiastical Union
World Wars with a final death struggle in Palestine

Any thinking, Bible-believing Christian can see how far the world has moved toward the fulfillment of these prophecies.

My father truly believed that his riches were in heaven and never wanted worldly possessions. He worked to make his family comfortable, but the real wealth he found was in the lives he changed.

I saw that man work until he would nearly drop, and yet I never heard him complain. If somebody called at one in the morning, he would answer and go wherever he was needed. Now that doesn't make him great because it's what he should have done by the way he believed, but it shows what kind of man he was.

Ralph Boyer could preach about the coming judgment of God and make people squirm in their seats. The next minute he could tell them about God's love and what He offered to every human being and how Jesus Christ was their Saviour—and suddenly they would smile and be reassured.

Dad put himself through Lebanon Valley College in Annville, Pennsylvania and was ordained. Over the years he was made an honorary doctor I don't know how many times, but he always hated to be called *Doctor* Boyer. He would say, when introduced that way, "My name is Ralph Boyer, glad to meet you."

His radio program, which he started in 1932, is still on the air in the same old time spot, 9 to 10 P.M. on Sunday evenings. When I was a kid he was also on the air every morning for fifteen minutes, playing records and talking about God to his radio audience.

He would take a newspaper and within five minutes relate stories to the Bible. Then with all his love and kindness he would come across to some guy going to work and say, "Are you burdened today? Turn your eyes upon Christ, give Him a chance in your life."

My father made me feel that the man who is really blessed is the man who is completely given to the will of God, completely given to the help of humanity, to God's power.

Eugene and Gerald had worked together in France prior to my father's death in 1965. Gerald played the organ and directed the music, and he also sang in French.

When Gene got to France he had to learn the language and he mastered it so well that today people don't even look upon him as an American. My two brothers went to France because they felt the need there for honest-to-goodness street evangelism. They felt the church was bogged down and they began pulling the crowds in. Gene and Gerry still are, and their ministry grows larger each day.

The point I am making is that my entire family was deeply religious, dedicated to spreading the word of God. Just before my grandfather died, for example, my father led him to Christ. Now Grandfather Boyer had never taken religion very seriously. He didn't try to stop Dad from going into the ministry, but he scoffed at the idea.

Well, about three months before he died, I remember my Dad came home one day with tears in his eyes. Grandfather had been ill, and when my father came into the house he said, "Daddy finally found the Lord."

I think it was one of my father's happiest days.

How did Joey Stevens come from this family?

2

I know who you are—you're the boy who sounds like a girl.

FROM THE TIME I was five years old until my voice changed when I was a teen-ager, I was what was known as a boy soprano. And that high-pitched voice got me into scraps on more than one occasion!

I remember once in a small rural Pennsylvania community I sang the Lord's Prayer. On this particular afternoon I hit a bad note. Remember that a boy soprano sounds like a girl to begin with, so when I muffed that note everyone raised their heads and my sister, Nancy, who stood right behind me in our family singing formation, started giggling. After the service we went outside and a wise guy—some kid a little older and bigger than myself told me, "I know who you are—you're the boy who sounds like a girl."

I hit him, and we got in a fight. Naturally my father reprimanded me as he had to do many times when I was a youngster.

Although the family was very religious, we kids were sometimes mischievous and naughty just like other children. Even in church we would start talking, or dropping hymn books, or writing notes to each other. All my father would have to do when he saw us start giggling was look down from the pulpit one time. Six kids would clam up quicker than you can say *Johnny Cracker.*

When Dad was spending most of his time in York preaching, we would have little Sunday night performances. Eugene, my oldest brother, was about thirteen at this time. After church we'd come home for the Sunday night *specials,* as we called them. Gene would come up with some wild costume or skit, and we'd play-act and ad lib the entire thing.

We were loose kids. I mean we liked to clown around, crack jokes, play pranks, and misbehave. The fact we were from a religious family didn't make us any different from other kids in that respect, but whatever we did was innocent fun. We never got into trouble with the law, or school authorities, or did anything to hurt anyone or damage someone else's property.

The Boyer Family would be hired to go to the various summer Bible camps in the Pennsylvania area. My father would do the preaching and we—the family—would sing. We had services in the morning and in the evening. Between times, we were free to do pretty much what we wanted in the way of camp activities.

We went to Red Rock Bible Conference near Berwick, Pennsylvania, and the Penn Grove Bible Conference, which my father later took over and ran for awhile, outside of York near Hanover, Pennsylvania.

The camp at Red Rock, however, was our favorite because we were sports happy anyway, and the camp there had everything—baseball, vollyball, swimming, football, just about anything we wanted.

There was a snack shop at Red Rock where the Boyer boys did their thing. By that I mean we would be the entertainers for the kids, doing little skits, or comic situations—like walking in the place like ducks. I suppose it was just the natural desire to entertain that made us do it. We were always on stage anyway so it seemed natural, therefore, to do some kind of entertaining when we weren't on stage.

As they say in show business, sometimes the things you don't plan—the impromptu situations—come off better than the productions. I remember one summer afternoon we decided to dress up like pirates and do a skit. Well, we didn't know what we were going to do except dress up like pirates.

So we came out ad-libbing and joking around, and finally laughing at each other to the point that everyone else started laughing. We bombed, but we really didn't bomb.

In attempting to describe my childhood I would have to say it was typical of what most people picture as small, country town life. The relationships between family members was very strong, not only because we felt a religious unity, but because in a rural setting where neighbors live miles apart, one has to depend on those in his immediate surroundings for companionship. There wasn't a street corner to hang on, so we did things together. We played and sang in a beautiful time of innocence.

These early years were wonderful years. There was a feeling of vitality because my father's ministry was growing daily. His children were healthy and growing up in an environment of spiritual guidance and parental love.

From the first to the eighth grade I attended the Pleasureville School, a four-room country school just outside of York. Each of the four rooms housed two grades, such as the first and second in one room, the third and fourth in another.

By the time I reached the sixth grade, I was very active in sports. Soccer was a popular game in the area, but most of the males in my family were avid football fans. My brothers taught me the fundamentals of the game, so when I got to the sixth grade, I began organizing a football team which the school consented to sponsor. The principal of our school helped us set up schedules by urging other schools to form similar teams. Eventually we formed a league, involving neighboring schools such as Ewingsville.

With the help of my older brothers, the Pleasureville School put together a T formation offense which I quarterbacked, and we developed a good variety of plays.

My brother Daniel would haul the team back and forth to the games in a big bread-loaf shaped bus that my father used in his ministry. Twenty kids would pile in the back of that bus and scream and yell their heads off as we headed to a ball game.

The Pleasureville School was about two and a half miles from our house. On nice days, I would ride my bike. When the weather was bad, when it was snowing or raining very hard, I would walk. I know that sounds like a typical story out of the country, but it's true. I either walked or rode my bike to school everyday.

These early days in the life of the Boyer family were some of the happiest of my life. All the kids were at home then, and my mother was in good health. By the time I reached high school she had to spend a great deal of her time in Philadelphia hospitals, this meant my father had to be there quite often himself; but when I was in grade school we were a tightly knit family. Whether playing football or praying at home, we did things as a family.

Every evening after dinner, my father would lead us in family prayer. We would stand or kneel together in the living room while my father read from the Bible or talked to us about the meaning of Christ. Then we would practice our family singing, or do homework, or practice our instruments. But whatever we did there was always that sense of unity.

I have always been an extrovert. Even back at Pleasureville School I took particular pains to see that my hair was combed just the way I wanted it, every strand in place. I would primp in front of mirrors at home and at school, and would wear sharp clothes. I wasn't especially cocky, but I did have a lot of confidence in myself and I enjoyed being in front of a group of people. I liked being the center of attention, and tried to put myself in that position whenever I could.

Throughout this period (during my last years at the Pleasureville School) my father's ministry was growing rapidly. His radio shows were becoming more popular and the ministers who came to his church seemed to be more prestigious as time went by. But even though my parents were so busy, they never neglected me. I can truthfully say I never suffered from a lack of fatherly and motherly love. Dad would take me to Philadelphia to see the A's play, and we went to all the football games. We finally met Joe Dimaggio at Shibe Park, and I guess it was the biggest day ever for the both of us. I didn't know it then, but Joe was to become one of my good friends later in life when I went to Atlantic City.

I can't remember a time in my life when I didn't like girls. Unlike most young boys before they reach the age of puberty, I had a fondness for girls. I enjoyed talking to them and liked to win their respect and admiration. Pulling pigtails wasn't for me!

Even in the fifth grade I had a girl friend named Anna Bailey. After we left the Pleasureville School I didn't see her again until I was in the tenth grade, two years later. I remember that night as if it were yesterday. I was playing with my band at the YWCA when I spotted her. That was one of the first times I ever got stoned on booze. And I did it just to prove to her what a man I was. I thought she would really think I was cool if she saw me getting drunk. I had to prove my manliness by being flipped out on alcohol!

There was a big teen-age club in York, which I began frequenting once I got to Hannah Penn Junior High School, where I attended ninth grade. It was sponsored by the local chapter of the United Fund and the place was huge, holding about 3,000 kids. By the time I was fourteen, I was in there every Monday, Wednesday and Saturday playing and singing with the band. It was while playing with this band that I developed a gang of followers, kids who would come just to catch my gig on stage. I did just what Elvis Presley did—the kind of thing that Tom Jones does now. I would sing blues in a style I developed by watching the bands that came through town, such as Lionel Hampton. One of my best friends during this time was Jesse Avery, a black kid who played a terrific tenor sax. He would teach me sax right out in the parking lot of school.

"Dig this, baby," he would tell me. "I just learned it down at Crispus Attucks. [a black youth organization]" And he'd blow some notes and I'd pick them up. I would also go to some of the black clubs with him to pick up on the sounds and the way they made them. I didn't attempt to sound like a black musician, but the black man has been in the forefront of the jazz movement in this country. It was through them that white musicians developed their styles.

The only way I knew to play was the down-home style—the low-gut blues. Now there was an era in jazz about this time when guys like Stan Getz and Zoot Sims were playing what they called *sophisticated jazz*—the cool soft sounds. And if you were a honker and played as crazy and wild as we did, you were out of it. We played rhythm and blues sounds like those of Flip Phillips and Illinois Jacquet, but our style fitted our audiences. We were known as the Purple Shirt Gang.

Billy Eckstein was the big vocalist at this time. *Mr. B* was the cool sound in singing in those days because Tony Bennett was just coming in and Frank Sinatra hadn't made his comeback. I used to sing all of Mr. B's tunes and I eventually picked up the same nickname.

Now the funny thing was that I didn't really have to drink or take drugs during this time to do my thing, but I thought it was cool because that's what other jazz people were doing. In fact, the first time I smoked pot was when I was fifteen. A chick turned me on to it and I wanted to look groovy to her—so I smoked it. Jazz and narcotics have always been closely associated, and I just thought it was part of the game.

During this period of junior high school and when I entered

William Penn Senior High School, I really began swinging out. There weren't enough girls to keep me happy. I dated most of them and loved every minute of it. In the seventh and eighth grades, my last two years in the country grade school, I had done a little necking in the clothes closet during the lunch periods, but I never did much formal dating. When junior high school rolled around, though, I began escorting girls like I had found a new world. I suppose I really had!

It was also in ninth grade that I got two other guys in my homeroom together and formed a group called the Jazz Trio. Junie Brown, John Loude, and myself used to stand around during noon recess and sing jazz. I remember that "Your Cheatin' Heart" written by Hank Williams and sung in a jazz style by Mel Torme, was a big tune at the time. So we'd get together and do it much in the same style that Ray Charles might do it now. We did other songs this way, just messing around in the school yard. The thing that put us together was that an English teacher noticed one day how the kids would gather around us to hear us sing.

"Why don't you try it on stage—you'd sound pretty good," he told us, so we decided to try it. We played a few assembly meetings and the teen club a couple of times. We'd do harmony and I'd do solos as well. It wasn't a bad group, really, considering we were amateurs and had little in the way of formal instruction.

I was never a violent kid and I didn't get into too many fights. But I was never afraid to stand up for myself even though I was smaller than many of the other guys my age.

I'll never forget an incident I had with a guy because I wanted to date his cousin, a beautiful girl from Dover, Pennsylvania. Her parents were from the old school. They believed a girl shouldn't go out of the house until she got married, but I had really flipped over this girl and carried a love for her until I got out of high school. She was gorgeous, with a beautiful face and wonderful figure.

Her cousin, the guy I got into trouble with, was a fellow who lived like the devil but looked like a saint in church on Sunday. Well, as it turned out, I wound up going out with his special girl one night and walked her home. It was all very innocent, but he got hot.

The next day as I was coming out of classes and heading home, three guys met me. He had sent them to get me but had not said who I was. He simply described me and told them where I'd be. Don't you know that two of the guys were black, and there wasn't a black guy in town who'd make a move against me? I was with them, playing their music, and we hit it off well. So when they saw who it was, one turned to the other and said, "Hey, it's Dave, daddy, what's this cat doin'? Dave's our man."

I told them to go back to the guy that sent them and tell him whenever he wanted a piece of me he could reach me at home or anywhere else he wanted. That was the end of that.

Throughout junior high school I got pretty good marks in my classes, but my father and I were already beginning to quarrel because I started coming in late. He also knew I had started smoking and was running with a fast crowd. We had a couple of arguments during those years. And the things I said to that man I wish I could apologize for now.

He would try to tell me of the dangers of drinking and running with wild crowds, but I would yell back at him as if he didn't know what he was talking about—and that man had worked with alcoholics and degenerates and godless people all of his life. He knew where I was headed, but there was nothing he could do to stop it. Here I was only in junior high school and already the signs were showing. Is it a wonder he was worried?

By the time I was a sophomore in senior high school, I was making the big move against my family's religious traditions. The world of music, booze, and applause and girls had gotten such a grip on me that by the time I was sixteen and able to get a license and play with union musicians, I was completely hooked on the whole scene.

It was during this time that I really had a couple of knock-down, drag-out fights with my father. On one occasion I actually cursed the dear man, telling him what he could do with his God. Like any sensible man, my father realized that every man is an individual with different drives, motivations and goals. He felt that the only way he could affect me was by the example he set—the way he lived.

More than simply preaching it, my father actually lived the gospel. And it was easy to see it working in him as a human being. Even to this day I find it was the example he set, the kind of life he lived, that influenced me finally to accept Christ as my Saviour. I simply could not forget the kind of life Dad lived, the happiness that filled his heart because he was doing the work of the Lord.

He could have come down hard on me, but that would only have made me bitter at him. He knew this, and that's why his approach was always one of love and understanding. To his credit, I have never forgotten his love. I went down a hard road, but when I came back again, I knew what that man had done for me and what he had meant to me. Had he not been the way he was, things might have turned out quite differently, for it has really been my father's teaching and his example that have gotten me through this life.

3

Joey Stevens—it sounded like a swinging name for a swinging guy.

DAVE BOYER really began emerging as Joey Stevens about the time I realized I had a singing voice that could turn people on. It first happened when I was in junior high school, playing football.

The team was supposed to put on a show for the school and the coach was looking for someone with a voice. When he asked for volunteers I stepped forward.

Now I had really been out of formal practice because I had all but quit singing with my family which was beginning to spread out at this time. Gene went to France, Dan went to college, Betty was married, and Nancy was also in college. Gerald was the only one still in high school.

We got the show ready to go and my number was a hit of the time, "Maybe You'll be There." I was on stage in the school auditorium dressed in my football uniform when I began belting that song. I got to the second bar and the girls started swooning and screaming. That was it. My mind clicked. Suddenly I imagined myself a Frank Sinatra—sharp clothes, big cars, tough chicks, the whole scene.

The first blast of air had been pumped into the ego of Dave Boyer —and Joey Stevens was conceived. He wasn't fully developed yet, but he was there.

From that moment on, all I could think of was singing. Football, studies and my family became secondary.

The next year Joey Stevens came to school looking the part he had made for himself: pegged pants, ducktail haircut. I really thought I was *it.*

I had no reason to put aside the religious training of my family other than the fact that I didn't want to subject myself to the discipline of Christianity. I felt that to get what I wanted and to go where I wanted—I just couldn't answer to God *or* to my parents.

I wanted to swing and I didn't have a care about anything else. That's what it came to, really. When I say swing I mean I felt I should be able to break God's laws about immorality and self-indulgence without anyone or anything telling me I shouldn't.

To me, marijuana was all right. If I wanted to get stoned on booze—that was my business. What I didn't want was parental or spiritual discipline guiding my behavior.

My falling away from my family and their life style really had little to do with them. It was no fault of theirs that I lost the faith they held so tenaciously. We always had communication, even though my mother was ill during my teen-age years and my father was a busy man. His work in the church kept him on the go day and night, and he frequently went to see my mother when she was in the hospital in Philadelphia. But even at these times my father would have breakfast with me in the morning and take me to school.

By the time I was 15, my gradual transition from the son of a preacher to a young kid who thought he knew all the answers and didn't need God to help him was just about complete. The whole concept of Christianity no longer had any meaning for me, so that when the split became complete—when I walked away from all my father believed in, from all I had been reared in—it was simply because I couldn't accept it. It stood in the way of my being the swinger I thought I was. It inhibited me from doing what I thought was the *in* thing. I felt religion was square by this time—corny—and I wanted no part of it.

Although Dad devoted as much time as he possibly could to bringing me up, the fact was that I was frequently alone. The family had begun to split up because the older kids were away at school, and my mother was frequently in the hospital. Added to this was the fact that my voice was changing from the time I was eleven until I reached the age of about fourteen, and my vision of the world outside was changing along with it.

I found out later from my brothers and sisters that I was the cause of great consternation to my parents. My mother felt particularly frustrated because she was in the hospital much of the time, and she felt helpless as far as offering me any guidance was concerned. She and my father would sit and discuss my behavior and what was happening to me, but about all she could do was pray. They spent a great deal of time in the hospital praying that God would lead me away from the life that I seemed headed for.

There were times when my father told me that I had to stop smoking and drinking. I was fifteen at the time, but already we were sneaking a beer or a drink when we could get someone to buy it for us. It was just a kick then, like that first cigarette behind the barn, but my father knew what was up, and he could see what was happening.

"It won't be just a couple," he said. "At your age it's a bad sign. Plus, you're under age. Think of the consequences of getting caught."

I would get angry when he said something like that. "It'll never grab me. I do it for fun," I would respond angrily.

My father was stricken with his first heart attack when I was fifteen. And I think it was then that I really realized just how deep the man's faith really was.

We were in Sunday School that particular morning, and I had gone to the rest room when someone came running in to tell me that something was wrong with Dad.

When I got to his side there was a glow of peace about him and he said to me, "David, not because of what you're doing [I was playing jazz with a group then—a pretty wild group] but I trust that you will come on my team."

"Well, maybe I will," I told him, but I said it because he was sick and I wanted to rest his mind—not because I really intended to change.

Finally he came to accept the fact that I would continue doing what I wanted to. He could see that I was bent on becoming a nightclub singer—a man about town—a good-time guy with the booze and the chicks. I think he finally accepted that no matter what he might do to prevent it, that's what I was to become. All he could do was pray for me, and he did plenty of that. I could also sense that he felt he had let me down. And I distinctly remember telling him on one occasion, "The reason I live this way is not because you failed me."

It would be easy for me now to say that I turned away from a godly life because of hypocrisy or a misunderstanding in the family —but that's just not the case. I saw hypocrites in church. We had fights at home, but there was no real environmental problem at all. Believe me, if more kids had parents like mine it would be a better world.

No, it was because I was more impressed with Satan's way than Christ's Way. That's what happens when you let the devil take a hold of even a small part of your life. First thing you know, he's got you in a trap you can't get out of. In my case, of course, I went along willingly enough despite the efforts of my God-fearing family who could see the snare I couldn't see. If they had mentioned the role of Satan in my life I would have laughed in their faces. This was the twentieth century! Satan belonged in the middle ages—or so I thought.

I was fifteen when I entered senior high school. Prior to this time, the union band people wouldn't listen to a kid, but they began coming to the senior high school dances and frequently invited me to play with them. I know on one occasion our band went to Wilkes-Barre, and we got home about four in the morning. My father, of course, was angry and asked me where I had been. I told him "out with some guys," which was a lie. I had been blowing with that union band, drinking and swinging all night. The next day Dad and I got into an argument and I wound up telling him I would do what I wanted and that nobody was going to stop me.

I went out for football in high school because I had been pretty good at the game in junior high school. I made the junior varsity squad and was scheduled to start in the first game as a T formation quarterback. Throughout the summer we practiced, and I thought I had it made until about a week before the first game.

I called a quarterback keeper play in practice one day, and got to about the line of scrimmage when a linebacker cracked through and nailed me hard. I felt something go, but I wasn't sure what it was. I found out seconds later.

On the next play, I was supposed to throw a pitch-out to a flanker back, but when I raised my arm to throw I knew something was broken. A pain shot to my shoulder. They found out later that I had broken my collar bone and I was put in traction. It was during the next five weeks when I was out of commission that I decided not to get hung up on football. Instead, I began concentrating on singing and playing and thinking about how much cooler it was to stand in front of a group of people—cigarette in hand and a drink nearby—and wail.

I learned to play my brand of sax—a hard swinging jazz style —from many of the good black musicians I worked with.

If I couldn't get pot before a gig, I'd get high on booze. And rather than stand up on stage and play it cool like Stan Getz, I'd blow "Hucklebuck" and roll around on the floor, kicking my feet wildly in the air.

And it was amazing the way I could turn a crowd on. I could play a jazz solo for a half hour—the sweat, the polka dot shirt, and the ducktail haircut, the boots, and the pants with the pegged legs and big knees—and the chicks would flip.

I really thought I was cool because the girls were beginning to come my way—even some of the nice girls came by on the sly. They'd never invite me home to dinner (not the nice girls), but they dug me. By this time I really believed that I was the coolest guy in school.

Ironically, I still enjoyed some of my classes. I got decent marks my first three years until the show biz thing became so dominant that I all but forgot the importance of anything else. By the end of my junior year I was doing badly enough to rate a summer school session. I picked it up well and, in fact, took a music theory course that really helped me. I also developed a little communication with the music teachers at school. They knew I had talent—if no self-control—and they gave me the extra attention that was needed to help me graduate my senior year.

It was during that final year of high school that I did the Paul Whiteman Show in New York—no small gig for a kid of seventeen from York, Pennsylvania!

Harry McLaughlin, a local newspaperman, had heard me sing at the teen center in York and at several other local functions around town. He wrote an article about me, and then contacted Paul Whiteman and set up an audition for me.

About two months after the audition, Whiteman scheduled me for an appearance on his talent scout show which was broadcast by radio throughout the country. Four of my friends and I drove up to New York for the show, and you could imagine how excited I was. It's hard to describe the sensation of waiting for the cue and knowing that in seconds people all over the country would be able to hear my voice. Oh, I was nervous, but my ego kept telling me *You'll knock 'em dead.* So the butterflies subsided when I began singing "How Deep is The Ocean" with Paul Whiteman's 32-piece band backing me up. I guess the whole town of York was tuned in for that broadcast and when I finished the show, the five of us went to Birdland to celebrate. It was there that night that I saw Billy Eckstein for the first time. I took in his marvelous voice while sitting at a table drinking whiskey sours.

The next day we piled in the car and headed straight back to York because I had to participate in a commencement show that was built around a Gay '90s theme.

One of my greatest thrills that last year of high school—aside from the Whiteman appearance, of course—was being asked to conduct the senior class choir.

I handpicked the best 150 students and used what funds I could muster to pick up some unusual choral arrangements. Well, it was a smash, to say the least, and even my father who was a hard man to impress with the show biz routine (particularly when he knew what it was doing to me) told me later. "You know, Dave, you can really conduct. I was surprised!"

One of the things that made the show so successful was that the late Spike Sprigle (who worked with many of the big bands during his career) helped me set up the arrangements and taught me some conducting techniques.

We did stuff ranging from Norman Luboff arrangements like "Laura," to a solo by me titled "Promise Me We'll Still Be Sweethearts After Graduation Day."

Before I graduated from William Penn Senior High School, Mr. Sprigle arranged for me to go to Ithaca College in Ithaca, New

York, which turned out to be a bomb because of my attitude. I never studied, but I did play with some good musicians and I met some extremely intelligent people and got on the intellectual kick.

This was my thing in college: drink booze, smoke pot, listen to records, talk about philosophy, and try to put the make on the chicks.

About the only courses I really gave attention to at Ithaca were my voice lessons. And I also studied piano fairly seriously but I just didn't take enough interest in the other courses to make any kind of grades at all.

One of the things that made it bad for me besides gigging with bands and all was that New York State law permits drinking at the age of eighteen. This meant, of course, I didn't have to make the effort of sneaking it, or finding someone to buy it for me, or being worried about getting caught by the police. Then, too, most other kids knew how to control it. They might drink at parties on the weekends or even have a couple of beers after class, but with me drinking was becoming an obsession even at this early stage of my life. To me it was cool to sit at the bar—not in the library.

Now I'd never credit myself with being an intellectual, but I did a lot of reading in those days, and it was heavy stuff—men like Voltaire, Spinoza, Nietzsche.

I attempted to make myself deny the concept of the Christian God because that concept didn't fit into the little world I was living in. It wasn't sophisticated. It was square—and square was the last thing I wanted to be. A knowledgable intellect (or so I thought) would think Jesus Christ is just another person—perhaps a great teacher. But a God? No. Absolutely not. So I began trying to make myself believe it. And this, coupled with the show biz syndrome and my growing desire to drink and smoke pot and take pills, began to turn Dave Boyer more and more into Joey Stevens.

This sounds weird, I suppose, but I distinctly remember walking through Ithaca one day, stoned on wine, and praying to the devil to take my soul. Today of course, satanic cults are common. This, I suppose, was much the same thing. But I was so caught up in this phony intellectualism and entertainment thing that I was beginning to really prefer Satan to God. Christianity would cramp my style. Satan wouldn't. So it was convenient to turn away from all the teaching I had received at home—from the fine example my family had set for me. Satan had suddenly become real to me.

I played fraternity parties that would last from Friday evening to Sunday afternoon—playing fourteen houses and never stopping. And the only way I could play that long—with only brief rest periods—was to stay zonked. Booze to get me high. Benny pills to keep me awake.

Not every musician needs that kind of stimulation. Take for instance the guy who ran the band I played in—Jerry Hallsband from New York City. He didn't need the booze. He got high doing his own real thing—playing. But I was popping pills and drinking anything I could get my hands on.

I remember Jerry came to see me after I started at the 500 Club in Atlantic City. He caught my first set, and then noticed that between sets I was really downing the booze.

"You've seen enough of those idiots drink to know what can happen. Don't let it happen to you Joey. You've got a great future if you can control yourself."

Well, that was about the whole scene in college. I played all weekend zonked out, so you could imagine the kind of shape I was in come Monday. Then there was the philosophical bit—the game so many kids play today. You arrive at the point where you think the world really needs your ideas. The humanistic attitude that leads you in search of utopia—and what eventually becomes an escape from reality.

After one year in college, I decided that studying wasn't for

Dave Boyer. My marks were bad and my heart wasn't in it. I decided then that my life had to be spent performing. I always had a natural performance gift anyway, and this is what really turned me on. I enjoyed everything that went with the entertainment profession. I liked people telling me they enjoyed my singing. And it was always fun to have a nice looking girl walk up and say she dug my act. After that first year, I left college and began singing and playing with various bands.

One night, I was dining at the Lincoln Woods Supper Club in York when the owner of the club asked me to sing. He had heard me perform in another club, and was anxious for his customers to hear me, too.

When I completed the first number, the crowd really let me know they appreciated the performance. I did a few more numbers and I went over so well that a few weeks later I was signed up as a regular act.

After I took that club job, I decided to change my name. Dave Boyer sounded a little square, I thought. I figured that a name with a ring to it would be more appealing. Also, I felt that using the name of Dave Boyer in a local supper club would hurt my father's work in the church. I might not have been on the same religious wave length as my father, but the last thing I wanted to do was hurt him. Besides, I didn't want to be known as a preacher's son.

I selected the last name of Stevens because a guy named Frank Stevens had been singing in the club before me, and I liked his voice.

When it came down to picking a first name, I wanted one that would picture me as what I wanted to be in life—a real swinger.

We went right down the list. Harry, Billy, Tom, Joey. That was it. Joey. Joey Stevens. I liked the ring it had. It sounded like a swinging name for a swinging guy. I could just hear a master of ceremonies in a big club somewhere bellowing:

"And now, ladies and gentlemen, we take pride in presenting that young, handsome, crooning sensation, Joey Stevens!"

I could see the blue pin spotlight hit me on the face as I walked out on stage to the cheers of the packed crowd.

In fact, when I looked in the mirror and saw an eighteen-year-old cat with a ducktail haircut, a big windsor knot tie, a one-button roll suit and pegged pants, I could see Joey Stevens staring right back at me.

Dave Boyer, the preacher's son, was gone. In his place stood an unbridled, wild, carefree Joey Stevens. I thought I had discovered true joy. Not only did I dig what I saw for the present, but also what it would bring me in the future. It was going to be one gigantic fun-time for Joey Stevens. Not for an instant did I ever reflect on what effect my new life might have on my parents or Dave Boyer, for that matter. I was only concerned about Joey Stevens—no one else.

4

The 500 Club was known as the "Showplace of the Stars."

WHILE I WAS at the Lincoln Woods Supper Club in York, the man who was handling my bookings at the time, Forrest Griffith, introduced me to Aldo Magnelli, a friend of his, who had come into the club to hear me sing.

After Mr. Magnelli talked to me, he and Griff, who was also from York, contacted Paul (Skinny) D'Amato, operator of the famous 500 Club in Atlantic City, New Jersey. I was overwhelmed when they made the call to Mr. D'Amato. The 500 Club was known as the "Showplace of the Stars" and it was Mr. D'Amato who helped team up Dean Martin and Jerry Lewis a few years earlier.

Besides this, Frank Sinatra, my singing idol, was a close friend of Mr. D'Amato's and had worked the 500 Club that summer. To think of singing on the same stage where The King sang just wigged me. Mr. D'Amato agreed to have me come in for a weekend in October. I couldn't wait for the day. Finally, when the time arrived for me to go, I was doubly excited because it was October 9, the day of my nineteenth birthday. I considered this a good omen.

Griff and I were going to drive down to Atlantic City on a Friday, even though I wasn't supposed to sing until Saturday night.

My father hadn't been too pleased with my working at clubs, and he wasn't very happy that I had changed my name; but when I prepared to leave for Atlantic City he said, "If this is what you want to do with your life, I can't stand in your way. You're making your own decision and both your mother and I love you, and we'll be praying for you." It wasn't the first time he had expressed those sentiments; nor was it to be the last.

Dad was always concerned about my drinking because of what it did to my two grandfathers before they found the Lord. He knew I had been drinking and smoking pot for about three years, and he felt that I would be even weaker to the temptations of booze and drugs if I were traveling around the nightclub circuit.

Early Friday morning, I kissed my parents goodbye, grabbed my two battered suitcases which I had packed the night before, and caught a bus to Griff's house. When I stepped off the bus Griff was already waiting outside in his car. I greeted him with a nervous smile, tossed my bags into the rear seat, climbed in next to him and said, "Let's get going."

We were on our way to Atlantic City, one of the world's greatest health and pleasure resorts. Situated on a narrow strip of land seven miles out from the mainland on the southern New Jersey coast, Atlantic City has eleven percent more sunshine than the average for the United States. And since I'd always been a sun lover, and one who could find peace of mind and relaxation by just basking in the sun, I recognized the climate would be ideal for me.

Besides a great climate, Atlantic City was the nation's leading convention city. The famous Convention Hall, home of the Miss America Pageant every summer, attracts hundreds of thousands of conventioneers each year. The convention delegates add a real air of frivolity to the "World's Playground" both summer and winter alike.

Of course the distinctive features of the town—besides its many fine amusement places, fine restaurants, motels, and hotels—are its seven-mile long ocean front Boardwalk and its clean beaches.

I could see myself spending afternoons on the Boardwalk

benches watching the girls go by, and mornings strolling along the beach by the oceanside. Then, too, they had fishing, horseback riding on the beach, and bike riding on the Boardwalk—in short, a kind of permanent vacation.

So when we crossed the Delaware River Bridge from Philadelphia over to New Jersey, I thought I could already smell the clean, non-polluted invigorating fresh air, despite the fact that we were still sixty miles from Atlantic City—sixty miles from a swinging show biz capital that attracted some 16 million visitors a year. And now Joey Stevens was going to make it 16 million and one!

(In my mind I felt that someday I'd be the most important visitor Atlantic City ever had, never realizing that I was like a Biblical lamb being led to the slaughter.)

When Griff and I got to town it was a clear, crisp October day. Not a cloud in the sky. Another great omen, I thought to myself.

Griff, sensing that I was anxious, looked over at me from behind the driver's seat and said, "Relax, kid, you don't sing until tomorrow, remember?"

I just laughed.

As soon as I walked into the 500 Club that afternoon, I felt a little tinge of disappointment. It wasn't at all what I had expected, but Griff reminded me that this was "only the afternoon and the club's empty." Well, it wasn't exactly empty. There were a few porters sweeping up and I was almost tempted to go over to one of them and proclaim, "Hey, I'm Joey Stevens. I open right here tomorrow night. If you're not doing anything, why don't you stop by and catch my act?"

Fortunately, I didn't utter a word to the porters. And it's probably a good thing. I might have wound up with a bucketful of dirty water on my head!

After surveying the club, I realized that it was too early to decide whether the 500 Club was everything I heard it was supposed to be. I had to wait only six more hours to discover the glitter and glamour of a big name supper club.

The 500 Club is located on Missouri Avenue in midtown Atlantic City in the heart of the town's after-dark bistro section. A short distance from the Boardwalk and beach, the Club was known as the "Showplace of the Stars" for good reason. In the early 1950s, when variety and talk shows weren't as predominant as they are on television today, the Big Five was the key entertainment spot.

All of the top stars, from Frank Sinatra on down, worked the 500 Club and were personal friends of its boss, Paul (Skinny) D'Amato. The really big stars had their footprints—and in Jimmy Durante's case, his noseprint—etched for life in the multi-colored concrete sidewalk in front of the club. In fact, outside of Grauman's Chinese Theatre in Hollywood, Atlantic City's 500 Club is the only other place that I know of that has the personal signatures and prints of so many stars on its "front porch." It serves as quite a red carpet for any prospective patron, and is a great conversation piece for the millions of vacationers who come to Atlantic City.

In those days, it was nothing to see forty or fifty chauffeur-driven limousines pulling up to the front door of the 500 Club to drop off men decked out in tuxedos, and women attired in expensive evening gowns and mink coats. The 500 Club was the epitome of a class supper club.

A gigantic sign over the entrance bore the inscription 500 CLUB. It was visible for blocks. Inside, the walls, tables, and booths—many of which were private—were designed in a unique zebra-skin motif. A cascading waterfall, with real water, gurgled on a specially built platform on top of the front door.

The front room of the club contained three large circular bars, seating about 100 persons each. There was an elevated terrace off to the side of the room and most of the celebrities would sit in the private booths in this location. And speaking of celebrities, there was a small bar aptly called the Celebrity Lounge. This separated the front room from the supper club (which seated 1000 persons) and was located in the rear. The Celebrity Lounge was the meeting and drinking place of night-life personalities, newspaper, television, and radio people. Naturally, there were plenty of celebrities who wanted to avoid the crowds in the front room.

Down a short flight of stairs from the Celebrity Lounge was the room referred to as the Little Five. Private parties and small banquets were catered in this room, the walls of which were lined with pictures of Frank Sinatra, Sammy Davis, Jr., Dean Martin and Jerry Lewis, the Andrews Sisters, Milton Berle, and Joe DiMaggio, a frequent visitor who became a close friend of mine. They had all been friends of Skinny D'Amato and had been at the club at one time or another. Most of them had been interviewed on a live radio show there hosted by Joe Pyne and Al Owen, local radio personalities.

Of course, a great thrill for me occurred the night that Skinny announced that my picture was going to hang on the wall next to all of these show-business greats. At this point, such a relatively insignificant thing as having my picture on a wall in a nightclub seemed like the most important thing in my life. I didn't stop to consider how this yearning to have my ego boosted could make me blind to the things of real value and meaning in life.

The big rear room of the club, where all of the stars performed, was the major attraction at the Five, however. It was a landmark. Thick, red wall-to-wall carpeting was on the floor and luxurious red velvet and satin drapes and tapestries adorned the walls. Skinny decorated the entire room himself and it was beautifully done. Even the curtains on the big stage were a deep red and one night, comic Milton Berle, who was then known as *Mr. Television,* came on stage to thunderous applause after I gave him an introduction, pulled down one of the curtains and caused me to yell in an adolescent shrill, "My gosh, you're tearing down the club!"

He wasn't, but his surprise opening had startled me so that he and I stood face to face on the stage for a full minute while the crowd choked with laughter.

Finally he blew a mouthful of cigar smoke in my direction and shouted, "Well, are you going to leave, or have I just gained a partner?" I left—the cigar smoke burning my eyes and the crowd's laughter stinging my ears.

As soon as I walked into the 500 Club that first night in town and saw those beautiful girls, that waterfall over the bar, those smartly attired men and women patrons, and heard the sounds of a good solid show band backing up a sophisticated revue, I believed that I had truly found my heaven right here on earth. Only later was I to discover that it was the beginning of my hell on earth.

Once inside the club that first night, I felt the York Gospel Center was a million miles away and as for Dave Boyer—who was he, anyway?

Then—unexpectedly—the big moment came. At the end of the first floor show of the night, I heard my name announced from the stage. It sort of stunned me. I wasn't supposed to sing until Saturday night!

"There must be some mistake," I whispered to Griff who was sitting at a table with me.

But apparently the comic on the bill who was doubling as master of ceremonies had received word that a new singer was in the audience, and he called on me to do a guest spot.

My knees were shaking as I prepared to walk the longest fifty feet of my life.

What a way to observe a birthday! I mused. Once on stage, I strolled over as casually as I could to Pete Miller, the club band-leader. I tried to muster up a confident tone as I leaned toward him and said, " 'September Song,' in C."

For it's a long, long time, from May to December. . . . The words seemed to flow. The audience, noisy at first, grew strangely silent. I didn't know if they were becoming attentive because of my voice, or my youth, or because I was new on the scene, but it didn't matter. They were listening.

After I finished "September Song," the crowd applauded vigorously. I couldn't believe it. Then one of the bartenders, Joe Camarota, began shouting,

"More, more!"

Another bartender, Patsy Wallace, took up the cry. And soon, the whole place came alive with the diners and drinkers screaming for another tune.

The butterflies I had in my stomach when I walked up to the stage disappeared. I looked at Pete Miller and grinned. He was smiling back at me.

"What's it gonna be, kid?" Pete asked.

" 'All of Me,' let's do it up-tempo in the same key," I shot back, imagining that might be the way Frank Sinatra would reply to a similar query.

". . . . you took the part, that once was my heart, so why not take 'All of me' ", I wailed.

When the song ended, the applause was deafening. People were standing and clapping their hands.

"It looks like you've got something going, kid," Pete Miller said to me. I took a bow, went back to my table and almost passed out from the excitement.

It had been my first appearance at the 500 Club and it had caught me by surprise. But I had been successful and the emotional drain left me speechless. I just sat at the table motionless, thinking that it couldn't be happening to me—but it was.

"Good job, Joey," Griff yelled, pumping my hand and pounding my back at the same time. About twenty minutes later, I had the opportunity to meet a man who has become a legendary figure in supper club and entertainment circles: Paul (Skinny) D'Amato.

Mr. D'Amato was impeccably attired and carried himself magnificently. He shook my hand firmly, sat down at our table, and spoke very softly to me. He made me feel at ease. He asked me questions about myself, and Griff told him that my father was a preacher. I was a little embarrassed at that—not that I wasn't proud of my father. It was just that I thought Mr. D'Amato might think I was a square and not want to hire me. So I smiled feebly and the subject changed.

As I later came to learn, Skinny D'Amato was more than just a great guy to many people, he was a great friend as well. A devoted family man, he and his wife Bettyjane, an attractive blonde ex-model, are the parents of two daughters, Paulajane and Cathy, and a son, Angelo. Paulajane, who eventually won the title of Miss Atlantic County and was a contestant in the Miss New Jersey Contest, is quite a singer in her own right and could well develop into a star.

Every Easter, Skinny put on a free matinee show for all youngsters, bringing in clowns, magicians, jugglers, and ventriloquists, much to the delight of the kiddies and their parents, too. And every Easter, from the time she was a little girl through her early teens, Paulajane and I would entertain the tots by singing and clowning around on the stage. Skinny and Bettyjane would get just as much kick out of our act as they did out of the biggest entertainers who worked the club.

Skinny is a great humanitarian—in fact, that word best describes him. He is always ready to help anyone. A guy who lost a job, someone who had been evicted, a fellow down on his luck—all knew that on Missouri Avenue was a man who was ready with a comforting pat on the back, and a few bucks in the pocket. It has been said that if Skinny D'Amato was ever repaid one-quarter of the money he's handed out over the years, he'd be a wealthy man. Always a sucker for a sob story, Skinny was considered the softest touch around.

I learned much from him. He never played position with people. Skinny didn't care if you were rich or poor, black or white— everyone was the same. I never saw him turn away anyone with a hard luck story. If there was a death and Skinny even remotely knew a member of the family, he would have his waiters and busboys bring all kinds of food—spaghetti, Italian bread, meat-balls, and lasagne—from the club to the home where the family was gathered. It was all gratis.

Skinny was an extremely dominant force in my life. Around the club, he watched over me like a hawk. He very seldom criticized me—but when he did—I listened. It was always constructive criti-cism, never something to hurt me. In a way, you might say I both loved and feared him—loved him because he was the classiest person I ever met—feared him because I was afraid of goofing up in front of him. But one thing for certain, I respected him tremen-dously, and not just because he was buddy-buddy with Frank Sinatra or ran an establishment that enjoyed a reputation of being an honest club.

When he excused himself from the table that first day after being introduced to me, Mr. D'Amato said, "Good luck, kid; and don't forget to see Pete Miller for rehearsal tomorrow."

Saturday and Sunday night both went very well. I worked the mammoth supper club in the rear; it was packed with convention-eers for the show. It was by far the largest club audience I had ever played, and it was a tough audience to impress. Convention dele-gates are out for a good time, usually. They laugh and shout their way through an evening.

"Joey Stevens, you've come a long way," I told myself.

And I certainly was as far away from my family's teachings as

I had ever been. I was naïve enough to believe that my shallow existence was the perfect life—that a life stripped of spiritual relationships could be meaningful. So I thought that I had really come somewhere—that I was on top of the world. But even in this shallow world I had some growing to do.

A few minutes later as I came out on stage to do my act, some conventioneers started yelling: "Bring on the girls!"

As a new act, I had to open the show and apparently a few of the delegates preferred a chorus line to a teen-age singer. But I didn't let the taunts of a few rowdies deter me from doing three numbers. And I must admit that the applause, while not as thunderous as the night before, was still gratifying.

After completing my last show that Sunday night, I went to get paid, and Mr. D'Amato handed me my salary. I thanked him for everything, and turned to walk out.

"Where are you going?" Skinny asked me.

"I'm going home, I guess," I said.

"You mean back to the hotel?" he questioned.

"No, sir, I mean back to York," I countered.

"Well, why don't you stay here for awhile?"

"You mean, why don't I stay here tonight?" I said, answering his question with another question.

"No," he said, "I mean why don't you stay here and work for awhile?"

It was then that I realized Mr. D'Amato, Frank Sinatra's pal, was asking me—Joey Stevens—a kid singer, to stay on as a singer in the 500 Club!

I was overcome. This was my first shot at the big time, really—Paul Whiteman's show included. It just didn't seem real, somehow. The 500 Club was in its heyday then. The entertainment roster was star-studded. I suppose I never really thought I would be up there with those people at that early stage in my career, but there I was anyway.

I accepted Mr. D'Amato's offer and left the club the happiest kid in the world.

Because I was so young, many of the artists used to play pranks on me.

ALMOST A WEEK after I opened, Looch Calabrese, a maitre d' at the club, sauntered up to me and said, "Say kid, have you ever emceed before?"

"No, I haven't," I replied.

"Well, you start tonight," Looch said.

This was another great break for me. It was a chance to broaden my entertainment scope and approach another avenue for bringing Joey Stevens to the limelight.

I was accepted by my peers around the club so much so, that I was often the brunt of practical jokes. These "rosies" were directed at me because I was the "resident kid."

One of the first rosies pulled on me at The Big Five involved two Runyonesque characters.

"Hey, kid," one of them growled at me out of the corner of his mouth as I came off stage, "come here."

"Yes, sir, what can I do for you?" I said.

"Look, kid," the other one snarled in a gravel-like voice, "you've been dancing with somebody's girl. And *somebody* doesn't like it. Do you get the picture or do we have to make it clearer than that?"

I got the picture, all right.

The *somebody* they were referring to was a pretty bad guy. Actually, I had danced with his girl earlier in the evening, but it was purely innocent. In fact, she had asked me to dance with her.

The two characters who confronted me knew that the dancing was innocent, but they figured they'd have some fun with me.

A few minutes later, I stepped from the stage after introducing a ventriloquist act.

"Joey, there's a long distance call for you in the phone booth," said one of the waitresses whom I had been dating.

When I picked up the phone, a raspy voice on the other end snapped, "Look, punk, if you don't lay off my girl, I'm going to mop up the street with you!"

As I started to speak, the receiver banged down in my ear and the line went dead.

"Hello, hello, hello," I murmured into the phone.

"I'm sorry, your party has disconnected," the long-distance operator said.

Terrified, I emerged from the phone booth. I felt like drinking a triple scotch, but I couldn't get it at the bar. Mr. D'Amato wouldn't permit me to be served because I was underage.

I didn't know where to turn. My legs felt watery. My head was light. Perspiration started to pour from my forehead.

Suddenly, one of the fellows who had given me the original warning "to lay off somebody's girl" was by my side.

"Hey, kid," he said, "take it easy, will you? It was all a joke. We were just kidding around. It was a rosie. Relax, will you? We didn't mean for you to take it so rough. Come on now, take it easy."

I didn't know whether to laugh or cry. So I did both. Tears poured down my smiling face, and I went to a bar up the street for a quick drink.

It may sound strange, but a pair of red flannel pajamas brought about a great deal of the good-natured ribbing I used to take around the club.

I brought the red pajamas with me from York. They were about as red as a fire engine and at least several sizes too large.

I was preparing to turn in for the night at the Penn-Plaza Hotel, a small, comfortable, family-type hotel located right down the street from the club, when there was a knock at the door of my room. Not too many people knew I was staying at the hotel. I was reluctant to say exactly where I was living because I needed my rest. I felt since I was working pretty hard around the club, my sleep was important to my general health, and especially to my voice. "You have to get plenty of rest," I would hear the great vocalists say when they worked the club, and I tried to abide by their advice.

So I knew that when I heard someone at the door at 4:30 A.M., it had to be a friend. It was Aldo Magnelli, the buddy of my manager Griff, standing at the door, a wide grin on his round face. Mr. Magnelli had been the guy who originally called Mr. D'Amato for me. He had driven in from his home in Harrisburg, Pennsylvania, for a short vacation.

"I just wanted to say hello and see how you're doing, Joey," Mr. Magnelli said to me as we stood at the door.

"Come in, come in," I muttered awkwardly, happy to see him, but suddenly conscious of the red flannel pajamas I was wearing.

Mr. Magnelli entered my tiny quarters, sat on a hard-backed chair in the corner next to the single bed, and exchanged pleasantries with me. We spoke about Griff, who would soon be leaving me as my manager, and then talked about happenings in and around York.

After a few minutes of chit-chat, I observed that Mr. Magnelli kept placing his hand over his mouth.

I didn't know if he was bored by our conversation and was politely attempting to stifle a yawn, or what.

It became embarrassing to both of us after a few minutes. By then Mr. Magnelli's hand was practically glued to his mouth. Finally, I couldn't stand it any longer.

"Mr. Magnelli, is something wrong with you?" I blurted.

He removed his hand from in front of his mouth, burst out laughing and shrieked, "No, Joey, something's wrong with you—those crazy red pajamas! Where'd you ever get those beauties?"

I admitted that I had bought them in York.

"Well I hope no one from the Club's seen you in them," he said, "or you'd never live it down."

After Mr. Magnelli left, I looked at myself from head to toe in the full-length mirror hanging on the outside of the closet door. And only then did I realize that the red pajamas were not merely outlandish in color, but also were so big on me that they actually covered my hands and toes. I should have told Mr. Magnelli, I thought to myself later, that I was going to wear them to play Santa Claus.

Apparently the sight of me in those flaming red pajamas was too much for him. Even though he had cautioned me about anyone from the club seeing me in them, when he returned to The Five, he related the tale to Mr. D'Amato who was sitting with a group of friends. They all broke up. And the news of my red pajamas spread like wildfire within minutes.

The next night when I appeared for work, Pete Miller, the bandleader, saw me in a hallway and said to me without a smile, "Did Joey get a goodnight's beddy-bye in those nice red pajamas?"

Johnny Civera, Pete's drummer, wanted to know if the "good fairy came around to see Joey and his pretty red pajamas last night."

It was too much. The bartenders, the hostesses, the waitresses, the busboys, some of the customers, the cigarette girls, Big Jim Grissom, the men's room attendant—they were all giving me the business about my red flannel pajamas.

The following day, I went downtown and bought another pair of flannel pajamas, but these were navy blue. I got rid of the red pajamas, but never heard the end of the hysterical stories, mostly of the myth variety, that were provoked by that one pair of red pajamas.

After a couple of weeks, Mr. D'Amato said to me, "Look, Joey, you don't have to keep calling me Mr. D'Amato—call me Skinny." This was another big thing for me, for it meant that I was on a first-name basis with the owner of a celebrated nightclub. I had truly arrived—or so I thought.

About the same time, Skinny started advising me about a number of things—from taste in clothes to stage presence.

"You've got to get rid of that ducktail haircut," Skinny chided me, adding that it made my hair look "too oily." "Besides it's 'way too long," he said.

Within minutes, he had Jimmy Ceres on the telephone (one of his friends and a gentleman who later toured with me when I worked clubs and did record dates throughout the country).

"Get Joey to Mike Civera and have his hair cut," Skinny told Jimmy. And though I inwardly regretted having my locks clipped, I obeyed Skinny's command. Several hours later I was a short-haired master of ceremonies.

Skinny didn't confine his objections to my long hair, however. He wasn't exactly choked up about my choice of clothes.

"What do you want to do, look like some jitterbug?" Skinny would say. "You have to have class, Joey. You're working club dates now. You have to dress like somebody."

On several occasions, Skinny accompanied me to a haberdashery in Atlantic City, and he would select and buy me suits, shirts, ties and cufflinks.

"And I don't want any of those pants pegged," he'd admonish the tailor who was fitting me.

During the next four years at the 500 Club, I had a ball. Besides appearing on the "Today Show" with Dean Martin and Jerry

Lewis, I introduced and performed with such stars as Frank Sinatra, Sammy Davis, Jr., Sophie Tucker, Jack E. Leonard (who became a close friend), Liberace, Patti Page, Al Martino and Vic Damone.

As I mentioned, Frank Sinatra had been my singing idol. So you can imagine how impressed I was to meet him and be able to present him on stage at the 500 Club. Skinny introduced me to him in his usual way, "Hey, kid," he said, "say hello to Frank Sinatra."

I'm sure Frank Sinatra thought I was just a little country boy because I stood there shaking his hand barely able to say a word.

"Glad to meet you, Joey," he said, "Skinny tells me you sing."

". . . er . . . er . . . I try," I said hesitantly, and managed a forced laugh.

"Well keep trying," he replied. "See you tonight."

Because I was so young, many of the artists used to play pranks on me. One night, Martin and Lewis were breaking it up on stage when they spotted me in the audience. I had developed a habit of introducing an act, then sitting at a ringside table to watch the performance. I found myself enjoying the shows as much—or more —than the patrons. Anyway, on that night, Dean and Jerry saw me in the crowd and called me back on stage. In a very serious manner Dean began praising me and talking about "what a promising young performer" I was.

I was flattered, indeed, but just before my head reached the point where it might have grown a size too large for my hat, Jerry sneaked behind me, poured a glass of ice water over my head, and with that, both Dean and Jerry started ripping my jacket off. As I struggled, Dean held me and Jerry loosened my shoelaces removed my shoes and tossed them into the hysterical crowd. It was all in good fun, they said later. And, reflecting on the incident, it really *was* fun.

One of the most memorable events during this period was doing the "Today Show" at the 500 Club with Dean Martin and Jerry Lewis.

It took place between 7 and 10 A.M. on Tuesday, June 26, 1956.

The show was billed as "TV's first early morning spectacular," and it was just that.

Among the stars on the show were Dean and Jerry, Faye Emerson, Lee Merriwether, Jack Lescoulie, Frank Blair and J. Fred Muggs, the lovable chimp.

At precisely 7 A.M. Jack Lescoulie announced over nationwide television, "Good morning, this is Today, June, 26." The theme music started, the 500 Club chorus line danced, and on a mike off-stage, I sang,

> It's show time on "Today," today
> So come along and join in the fun
> It's fun time on "Today," today
> The whole gang is here, all but one,
> We'll bring you the news
> And the temperatures too
> And show you some talent
> Some old and some new
> It's show time on Today you know
> So let's get on with the show. . . .

After a drum roll, I proclaimed,

"Presenting—from the famous 500 Club in Atlantic City, New Jersey, TV's first early morning spectacular and introducing America's Number One introducer, *Mr. Jack Lescoulie!"*

When Lescoulie began to tell a joke, he was interrupted by music and following another drum roll, I said, "And here—in place of the vacationing Dave Garroway—is the pride of Beaumont, Texas, Miss *Faye Emerson!"* I then introduced "an orchestra conductor of great renown, the leader of the Charleston Charlestonians, Mr. Frank (Curley) Blair."

My next introduction was for "a young lady whose fame started right here in Atlantic City as the winner of the Miss America Contest—*Miss America* of 1955, Miss Lee Merriwether!"

Another drum roll and I announced, "And last, but certainly not least, the bon vivant of show business, the wit of all wits, Mr. *J. Fred* (he kills them at Lindy's) *Muggs!*"

Then Faye took over and said, "Yes, it's show time on 'Today,' today as our show originates from the famous 500 Club in Atlantic City, New Jersey. On our program this morning you will meet Miss Mona Carol, a pretty young recording artist, Miss Joan Kayne, a wonderful dancer and former Miss New York City; the fabulous Joe Mays Quartet; a brilliant young man, eighteen-years old, Mr. Pippy Walters; a tremendous young showman of twenty years, Mr. Joey Stevens; some famous people at our ringside tables, and the one and only team of *Dean Martin* and *Jerry Lewis!*"

My heart swelled with pride when I heard myself described as "a tremendous young showman" on national television. Besides, it would be another line to throw to the chicks that I was chasing at the time.

But a bigger moment was yet to come for me. After about the first half hour, Faye Emerson introduced me, and I, Joey Stevens, right there on the stage at the 500 Club, right there on nation-wide television, sang a solo. The song was "Ebbtide," and when I finished, I was numb. Then Lee Merriwether, Miss America herself, joined me on stage to sing a duet. What a gas!

After Dean Martin and Jerry Lewis broke it up on stage for a solid hour, there were the usual runs of commercials and station breaks.

When the three-hour show ended, we were all called on stage and Dean and Jerry continued to clown around as we signed off.

Few in the audience—in fact, even few in the cast—knew that Dean and Jerry weren't talking to each other off stage when that show was telecast. In fact, the "Today Show" was to be one of their last appearances as a team. They split up shortly after their engagement at the 500 Club, and each became a star in his own right.

When veteran comedian Jack E. Leonard was topping the bill at the club, he turned the tables on me. After I introduced him, I went to a ringside table to watch. When he finished, I went back on stage to sing a few numbers with the band.

As I was singing, I glanced down at the remaining crowd—most of them had left after Jack had finished—and much to my amazement, there was the chunky comic seated at ringside.

When the show ended, Jack, who is noted for his quick and biting humor, came up to me backstage.

"Hey, you little squirt," he snapped. "You have a nice voice for a kid, but for Pete's sake, lower the mike so the people can see who you are." I took his advice.

From observing such superstars as Frank Sinatra and Sammy Davis Jr., I learned that even they put a great deal of hard work and effort into their nightclub acts. I decided that I had to do the same.

It might seem like a cliche, but I can truthfully say the bigger the star, the more gracious he is. At least that's the way it appeared to a very young Joey Stevens who was then at an extremely impressionable stage of life. Trouble is, most of the things impressing me then were the very things that later led to my downfall.

To further inflate my ego, I always thought myself a big shot to be invited by Skinny and some of his friends to drive up to New York for lunch every so often.

The high point of our trip would be stopping at Toots Shor's Restaurant and Lounge on 52nd Street. New York always fascinated me, even when as a youngster I went there with my family.

But traveling with Skinny and the guys to Toots Shor's made me aware of how much I had changed since my childhood.

Once I considered the Empire State Building and the Statue of Liberty the greatest sights New York had to offer. But sitting in Toots Shor's at the same table with celebrities made me forget there were any other attractions in New York. They were there all right, but I was missing them and a lot of other things in life.

Like Skinny, Toots Shor is a legendary host—a roundfaced, cheery man. One of his trademarks was his penchant for ridiculing his guests. The more prominent they were, the more he needled them. Broadway saloon columnist Earl Wilson, whose widely-read column is syndicated in newspapers throughout the country, would frequently write about the latest actor, singer or sports figure whom Toots insulted by calling him a *crum-bum* or a *creep*. But in reality, the targets of Toots' verbal barrages knew that he only singled out those he admired.

It got so that if Toots Shor didn't call you a crum-bum, you hadn't yet arrived in Broadway circles.

Not only was Toots extremely close to many celebrities, but he also drank with them. Autograph seekers who wanted to catch a glimpse of the top entertainment personalities could catch them bending elbows with Toots just about any day of the week.

One of Toots' greatest traits was picking up the check for ex-stars whose careers and bankrolls were on the wane. One afternoon when I was there, Toots spotted a former child actor who had hit the skids. Toots tottered over to his table, joined him for lunch, invited him and his family back for dinner, picked up the check, then slipped him $100 "for cab fare." He had made the ex-star feel like a headliner again. But that was just one of many such incidents in Toots' life.

One afternoon, a bunch of us who had motored up to New York from Atlantic City with Skinny were kidding around with Toots at his table. Skinny excused himself to talk to some friends in another part of the cocktail lounge. Suddenly Toots, whom I didn't really know that well at the time, turned to me and said, "Come on kid, have a few drinks with us."

At that time, I had never had even a sip of wine in front of Skinny. I respected him too much. But now, with Toots asking me to join him and the boys for a drink, I didn't know what to say. I wanted to be accepted by Toots, but didn't know what Skinny's reaction would be if he came back and saw me drinking.

I guess I hesitated long enough for Toots to figure out what was troubling me.

"Don't worry about Skinny, he's not going to spank you," Toots chided me. "Besides," he added, "all the great singers drink. They need it to pep them up. Anyhow, it's good for their voices. Makes their vocal chords relax."

That almost convinced me to sneak a taste, but when I saw Skinny walking back across the room to our table, I mumbled some kind of apology like, "Thanks anyway, Mr. Shor, but I have sort of an upset stomach now."

Toots laughed, said he had just been "fooling around," then told Skinny who had returned, that I had tried to order a drink just as soon as he slipped away from the table, but that he wouldn't serve me because he didn't want to ruin my voice!

I never had the distinction of being called a crum-bum by Toots Shor, but I've always admired him anyway.

I left the Penn-Plaza Hotel near the 500 Club and moved to the Ambassador Hotel on the Boardwalk, which is the largest hotel in Atlantic City, with 700 rooms. During the off-season, the Ambassador offered bargain rates so I decided to take advantage of living luxuriously in a beachfront hotel.

As it turned out, I almost was evicted the first week I checked in. When I'd return from the club during the early morning hours,

I'd play my Frank Sinatra, Tony Bennett, Eddie Fisher or Pat Boone albums to try to study the way they sang. I paid particular attention to their phrasing and made an attempt to learn a little something from each of them.

Apparently, my neighbors in the rooms surrounding mine weren't that eager to hear Frank, Tony, or Eddie at 5:30 in the morning. They started calling the desk clerk to complain. After he'd call me, I would turn the volume down, but for some reason, it never seemed to satisfy the other hotel guests. Finally, after explaining to the desk clerk that I was a singer and had to listen to these records to study voice, I agreed to restrict my record-playing to the late afternoon. It didn't help. I still had complaints about the sounds coming from my room, so I had to discontinue playing the records, or find myself out of the Ambassador.

About two weeks after I had stopped playing the records, I picked up a new Sinatra album in town. It was called *Come Fly with Me* and was supposed to be a real swinging record. I couldn't wait to get it home to play it, but then I remembered that I had promised I'd curtail my record playing.

It was early evening when I returned to my room. I was going to shower, shave, comb my hair, and get ready for work. Then I saw my phonograph on a table in the corner. I couldn't resist the temptation. Anyhow, it was only about 8:30, so I didn't think anyone was bedded down for the night.

I took the record out of the album jacket, placed it on the turntable, and switched it on. Sinatra was singing about flying away with him, and I was digging every sound. A knock on my door interrupted my mood. It was the guy next door.

"Look," he started out, "I don't know you, and you don't know me, but I've been complaining about you since you moved in here. I have nothing personal against you, buddy, but I drive a moving van and have to get my sleep whenever I can. Will you do me a favor and break that record, or shut it off and let me get some sleep?"

He whined his request so sympathetically that I quickly turned off my new Sinatra record. (I sure wasn't going to break it.)

I moved out of the Ambassador a couple of weeks later and took an apartment in the Inlet section of town, about 15 blocks from the Club. I was always conscientious about my job. Once, when I was living in the apartment, there was a blinding snowstorm. Atlantic City usually has only about one snowstorm a winter, but this one was a lulu. It dumped about twenty inches of snow on the ground, and the whirling, blizzard-like winds had created enormous snow drifts in the unprotected Boardwalk area where I lived.

I was supposed to be to work about 9 P.M. When I looked out my window at 7:30, I could see nothing but white. Snow was piled everywhere. I tried to open my front door, but the snow was piled so high against it the door wouldn't budge. I went to the back door where the snow wasn't so deep, borrowed a snow shovel from a guy next door who must have thought I was crazy when I told him I was going to dig myself out to go to work.

"You gotta be kidding," he said to me on his back porch stairs as the wind howled around us. "No one's gonna be in the club tonight, Joey."

"Well, I am," I told him, thanking him for the shovel.

Around 8 P.M., I started digging a path from my front door to the street. At 8:45, I had made enough of a dent in the snow to be able to make it from my apartment to a taxicab. My nose was beet red, my fingers felt like they were going to come off, and my ears were ice cold. I went back into my room to call a cab, but the lines must have been down. The phone was dead.

Determined to make it to work, I could think of no other way to get there but to walk. I didn't have any boots, so I wore a pair of galoshes, three sweaters, a beat-up raincoat and a pair of dry dungarees and started out on my 15-block jaunt. I felt like Admiral Byrd at the South Pole. Electricity was out in many sections of the city. There was no traffic and I didn't see a soul on the street, but I plodded on. I knew that I had a fresh change of clothes at the club, so the only worry I had was getting there on time. The clock in a jewelry store window read 9:05 and I was still about 10 blocks away. Just then, a police car came around the corner and one of the patrolmen asked me if I needed a lift. I think I was inside the prowl car before I had a chance to answer.

I was about 15 minutes late for work, but there were only a half dozen persons sitting at the bar in the club when I arrived.

"Where you been, Joey?" Skinny asked me.

"Gee, I'm sorry I'm late, Skinny," I said, "but I couldn't get out of the apartment because of this blizzard."

"Yeah," he replied, "well, we've been trying to call you to tell you not to bother to come in, but the phone must have been out of order. Tough break, kid, you could have had yourself a night off, but as long as you're here, you might as well do a few numbers."

"But, Skinny," I said, "the band didn't show up. Who's going to accompany me?"

"Oh, I forgot to tell you," he answered, "we called them and told them to forget about coming to work. Their phones weren't out of order. So just sit down at the piano and sing a few songs. You can play the piano, can't you, Joey?"

"Well, not really, but I suppose I can fake it," I said.

Apparently I must have faked it pretty well, because the small crowd applauded me vigorously. Of course, they might have been clapping their hands to keep warm, since the heating system at the club had gone on the blink!

One of my kicks during this period was entertaining young children confined to institutions. I have always loved kids, and I was delighted to perform for the youthful patients in the Atlantic

City Hospital and Shore Memorial Hospital pediatric wards; and for the Betty Bacharach Home for Afflicted Children, in Longport, and the Children's Seashore House in Atlantic City.

I once told a reporter who was interviewing me that working in the crippled children's wards appealed to me more than doing the same act on stage for money. And I was sincere when I made the statement. When civic groups asked me to do a show for bedridden youngsters, I felt it was an opportunity, rather than an obligation.

Marie McCullough, director of the Atlantic City Models' Guild and a civic leader, once arranged four benefits for me in one day.

"Now I know it's practically impossible, Joey, but we're counting on you so much," she said. I tried to explain to Marie that there was a large convention in town on the day she had scheduled the four benefits and that I would be putting on four big shows at the club that night. I asked her if she minded if I passed up at least one of the benefits and she replied, "I won't mind, but think of those children who want to hear you." That was all she had to say. I did a total of eight shows and enjoyed every minute of each one of them.

Upper left: I was a happy little guy. *Upper right:* At Hannah Penn Junior High School, Hal (Junie) Brown and I were both quarterbacks. He was one of my best friends.

When I was about 12, the whole family performed at the York Gospel Center: (left to right) Daniel, Gerry, me, Pop (Mother and Nancy seated), Betty and Eugene.

The 500 Club of Atlantic City—the Showplace of the Stars. That's the NBC-TV camera truck preparing for the "Today Show" telecast at the time I was MC and a featured entertainer at the club.

Here I am with some fellows I worked with: me, Comedian Richie Forbes, famed TV and movie comic Jack E. Leonard, and behind Jack E., Joey Villa, other half of the Forbes and Villa team. *Below:* Taken at the 500 Club. Paul (Skinny) D'Amato, club owner, seated, is flanked by me, Joey Stevens, and Pete Miller. (In those days I thought I could handle liquor.)

Pip Walters (my partner) and me.

I traded my tux for one of Uncle Sam's suits. Here I'm singing with the Third Army Dance Band. *Below:* Joey Stevens returned from the service and singing a duet with Lee Merriwether (Miss America).

Above: The entire cast of the "To-day Show" on stage at the 500 Club. It was a great thrill to take part in this telecast, which was one of Martin and Lewis's last shows together as a team. *Right:* So long Joey. Dave is back and gigging for God.

6

I never felt so humiliated in my life.

IN 1954, I MADE a record titled "Tell Me You're in Love," a romantic ballad. I recorded it on the B.B.S. label for a fellow by the name of Bill Borelli who had been a coauthor of the song.

We recorded the tune in a New York studio with a fifty-piece band conducted by Joe Leahy. Al Martino's first big smash "Here in My Heart" was also produced and written by Bill, and helped convert B.B.S. into a major company among the independent labels.

"Here in My Heart" was an immediate hit. It was number one on the hit parade charts for many weeks, and turned him from an obscure club singer into a nightclub entertainer who commanded top billing and a salary to match.

The guys around the 500 Club felt that what had happened to Al Martino could happen to Joey Stevens. With this in mind, we cut "Tell Me You're in Love," and, accompanied by my good friend, Jimmy Ceres, also from the 500 Club, we embarked on a tour of fifty cities, plugging the record on disc jockey shows and making personal appearances wherever possible.

Everywhere we went, we were haunted by Al's record of "Here in My Heart." It was being played on juke boxes, on the radio, and on television, and just about everytime I heard it I'd turn around to Jimmy and say, "Boy, if I could only have one-tenth of the sales and plays that Al Martino's had from his record, I'd be a real happy guy."

Everytime I made that remark, Jimmy would laugh uproariously and say, "Yes, and you'd be a real rich guy, too."

Jimmy Ceres was really quite a character. A former barber from Northern New Jersey, he was a rough, raucous, powerful, lovable guy, whose bark was much worse than his bite. As boisterous and rowdy as Jimmy could get, he had a tender streak that ran the entire length of his back. He was my protector and treated me as a father treats his son. Traveling with Jimmy Ceres on the road was an experience I'll always cherish.

One of the big stops on our tour was the National Music Operators' Association Convention in Chicago. Jimmy and Bill felt the convention would be a great showcase not only for Joey Stevens —but my record as well.

All the big names in the recording industry were on hand at the convention. There were disc jockeys, record producers, technicians, juke box dealers, song promoters and writers—virtually anyone who had a say in what music lovers listened to and bought.

But in addition to the presence of these key industry people, the highlight of the convention was the appearance of the major recording artists. Most of the biggies were on hand to sing for, and personally shake hands with the industry's top brass.

Tony Bennett was there riding the crest of his tremendous favorite "There'll Be No Teardrops." Eddie Fisher, who was at the peak of his success, was also there plugging several records he had recently made.

Here I was hobnobbing and exchanging stories with the stars, but my own big moment was still to come.

We were staying at the Palmer House, one of Chicago's most luxurious hotels, and many of the recording artists, disc jockeys and executives were also staying there. Because I was so young, and relatively unknown, I always left big tips in restaurants. I suppose in those days I sought recognition, and even though I probably wouldn't be seeing most of the waiters or waitresses that served me again, I wanted to feel like a big man—so I overtipped.

Now, staying at the Palmer House, I felt I had to keep up with the Tony Bennetts and the Eddie Fishers who were there. I wanted the busboys, the room clerks, the maids, the doormen—everyone —to remember Joey Stevens as being a liberal, generous tipper. No small-time country bumpkin stuff for me—I was a Rockefeller in disguise! And even though I really didn't have the money, I tipped like a millionaire.

It was at the Palmer House that Jimmy Ceres really blew his top with me about my bad habit of overtipping.

I had about six bucks in my pocket one night, and the check for coffee and cake came to a couple of dollars. I noticed a large crowd of prominent entertainers had flocked around the table next to ours.

"Here, let me take that check," I said to Jimmy in a voice loud enough to cause the heads at the next table to turn.

"Okay, Joey, it's yours," Jimmy said, realizing that the check was only for a couple of bucks.

As the waitress came back to our table to pick up the money, I gave her the deuce, and then squeezed my remaining four dollars into her hand.

"Here, dear," I said in a grandiose tone, "the service has been great, and you've been so sweet—here's a little something for you."

The poor chick was so startled, she dropped the four bills on the floor.

"What is this, some kind of gag?" she asked disgustedly. "You know, you entertainers are all alike. Very funny. Well, I don't appreciate getting play money, especially from a cheap creep like you." She left in a huff.

The blood rushed to my face. I turned all shades of red. I tried to catch her and to mutter that the money was real, not fake, and I truly was tipping her four dollars, but the words just didn't come out of my mouth.

Meanwhile, since I had made such a production out of the whole incident, everyone at the next table was staring at me. I never felt so humiliated in my life. The people at the other table just tittered, but Jimmy Ceres was laughing.

"Maybe that'll teach you a lesson, wise guy." Jimmy roared, as everyone in the restaurant turned in our direction. "You can't tip like you're the richest guy in the world. You're just a normal kid and feel sorry for everyone because your father's a preacher, and he's always worried about the working people. But you have to learn to take it easy. You don't have the money to be burning it the way you do."

My eyes were tearing as we walked from the room. I could feel the stares of what seemed like thousands of people on me as I made my exodus. Since that experience, every time I'd reach into my pocket to overtip, I'd think back to that embarrassing moment. But if Jimmy was with me, I didn't even have to think back—because he'd give me a nudge. And a nudge from Jimmy Ceres felt like a poke by Rocky Marciano.

I never thought I'd live down my humiliation at the convention, but, fortunately for me, I did—the next night.

Many of the stars had been called on to sing their record hits in front of the disc jockeys.

Now it was my turn. I was to sing my recording of "Tell Me You're In Love", but surprisingly, following Tony Bennett and Eddie Fisher on stage didn't shake me up too much. I believed the record was good, the arrangement good, and my voice was okay. After I sang, I got a nice round of applause, but the fun was just starting. When Jimmy and I went to the Palmer House Cocktail Lounge after my number, a group of deejays came over to shake my hand. They were all saying how great the number sounded, and they promised they would play it on their shows. I was feeling terrific.

A little later, some wealthy industrial tycoon came over to Jimmy and me, introduced himself and then leaned over and whispered to me,"Who's this guy with you?"

"He's my road manager," I told him.

"Well, is he doing you any good, kid?"

"Sure he is. Why do you ask?"

He answered that if I "hung around Chicago," he'd get me "all the work and all the breaks you need to become a big star."

He then slipped me a key to a private club in Chicago, told me to get rid of Jimmy, and to meet him there later so we could "discuss the matter."

I said, thanks, but no thanks. I told him I enjoyed working at the 500 Club, and didn't want to leave Atlantic City. He said he understood, but that if I ever changed my mind, I'd always have work around Chicago.

After we left Chicago, we came back East to promote the record. We were going to try to follow up on the success we had enjoyed at the convention. Our first stop was West Point, New York. Because I had been a tremendous fan of Army's famed Glenn Davis-Doc Blanchard football powerhouse, I got a special bang out of our visit there.

Jimmy and I stayed at the Hotel Thayer, the same hotel where the guests of most of the Cadets stopped when they were in town. I did a couple of teen-age record hops and appeared on a few radio

shows in the West Point area. The act seemed to be going over
relatively well. My picture was on posters around town, and my
name was in the local papers and on the radio. When one of the
girl friends of a cadet heard that I was staying at the Thayer, a
group of cadets and their girls dropped by the hotel, more out of
curiosity than anything else. It just so happened that the night they
came in I was in the hotel coffee shop getting a bite to eat with
Jimmy.

"There he is," a blonde-haired girl of about seventeen squealed.
Then they charged over to me like I was some kind of singing idol
and asked for my autograph. I thought they were just clowning
around or teasing me at first, but then I saw they were serious—
and determined. I obliged, but had to turn them down when they
pleaded for me to sing "Tell Me You're in Love" which was really
getting a lot of air play in the area because of my saturation
promotion campaign.

"I can't sing it," I apologized, "I don't have any accompaniment, but thanks anyway for the request."

The group groaned, and I turned around to go back to Jimmy
at the table when I felt a firm grip on my right shoulder. I spun
my head around, looked up about a foot and gazed directly into
the steel gray eyes of a muscular, ferocious looking cadet who
looked like he played the entire left side line of the Army football
team.

"You don't need any accompaniment. Sing!" he commanded.

I sang.

Little did I know that Tyrone Power, who was making a movie
there, and several of the actors and actresses who were on location
shooting the picture had walked in during the middle of my conversation with the cadets and their girls and had heard me sing.

When I finished I received a big hand, a few slaps on the back, a *thank you* from the gorilla who had "encouraged" me to sing, and a handshake from Ty Power. He complimented me on the way I handled the situation, said he thought my voice sounded good, and that he felt I had a lot of personality.

"You should go a long way, son," the handsome actor said to me. Then, with a laugh, he added, "As a matter of fact, you look a lot like Pat Boone."

"Yeh," I shot back with a grin, "the only thing I need are Pat's white bucks and Pat's money."

We wound up a promotion tour in Pennsylvania. In Harrisburg, the state capital, I crossed paths with another Hollywood actor, Jeff Chandler. The rugged, prematurely gray-haired actor had just cut a record and was out on the road plugging it. We were both guests on an afternoon radio show, and after we got through I spoke briefly with Jeff who had to rush to catch a plane for New York.

"You have the potential to go all the way, Joey," he told me. "But don't forget, it's hard work and it won't come overnight."

About a week later, I arrived at a Pittsburgh radio station studio and was greeted by—Jeff Chandler! "What are you doing—following me?" he asked in his deep, resonant voice. He was about to leave the studio, but paused long enough to say, "Remember what I told you last week about being a star? Well, don't forget that it all depends on how good you are."

I've never forgotten the words of advice that I received from Jeff Chandler. And though we spent only a few minutes together during our two chance meetings, his words of wisdom haunted me, and seemed to grow more meaningful after I learned of his tragic death while undergoing surgery for a back ailment.

Financially and artistically, my recording of "Tell Me You're in Love" met with only a modicum of success. I suppose I only sold a couple of thousand copies and had plays on a few hundred juke boxes, but the experience I gained on our promotion tour—and the people I met—did me a world of good in the entertainment field.

7

If there's such a thing as love at first sight, it happened to me.

ONE SPRING AFTERNOON in 1957, Skinny told me, "There's a tap dancer working on tonight's show. I want you to watch him carefully and tell me what you think of him. I have an idea."

I didn't know it at the time, but Skinny's idea was to team up the tap dancer, Pip Walters, and me. After all, Skinny helped to put together Dean Martin and Jerry Lewis, so why not Pip Walters and Joey Stevens? As a matter of fact Pip had appeared on the "Today Show" with me, so he was no stranger.

I caught Pip's act that night. Not only was he a superb tap and acrobatic dancer, but he was also a skilled comic. I liked what I saw, and shortly afterwards Skinny teamed us up and became our personal manager. Pip would dance and clown around, while I would play my horn, sing and do impressions. It was a groovy act.

After breaking in the act at The Five, Skinny, acting as our manager, contacted other clubs around the country and arranged for us to appear in them. We played some top spots in the East and success appeared to be rolling our way when Uncle Sam stepped into the picture.

We had closed the Horizon Room in Pittsburgh to standing ovations, and were preparing to move on to New York when it happened in July, 1957. I used to call Skinny every night from the road to tell him how we were doing. Of course, I never mentioned the liquor and pills that were more and more becoming a part of my life.

I was only a teen-ager when I started at the 500 Club, and Skinny wouldn't permit me to drink there. When he found out I was smoking a little pot, he really blew his top.

"You either drop that stuff, kid, or you go."

I didn't completely drop it, but Skinny never knew it. So for the next couple of years I was what you might describe as a social drinker. Oh, I got stoned once in a while, but I was staying in pretty good physical shape.

By the time we started our road trip, however, I was becoming something of a lush. Skinny wasn't around to keep me in tow and I was gradually becoming more dependent on the use of alcohol and drugs to do my act.

After we took our equipment out of the Horizon Room and packed it for shipment to our New York engagement, I telephoned Skinny in Atlantic City. I was in great frame of mind, because our act was really beginning to jell. The reviews of our Horizon Room stint were fantastic. *New York here we come,* I thought to myself as I waited for the long distance operator to get Skinny on the phone.

I'll never forget that conversation.

"Hello, Skinny, it's Joey," I said. "We did terrific tonight and they want us back for three weeks when we close in New York," I added excitedly. Then there was a pause.

"Skinny . . . Skinny . . . Hey, Skinny, are you there? Is something wrong?"

"Kid," Skinny began softly. "You got your draft notice in the mail today. You have to go next month—so you better come on back to Atlantic City."

At first I thought Skinny was playing a rosie on me, but then I realized he wouldn't joke with me about something as serious as my career. Besides, he sounded too somber on the phone to be kidding around.

I was at a loss for words. It was as if Jerry Lewis had poured a whole tub of ice water on me, and not just a glass as he had before. I was stunned, upset, and a little frightened about my future. I broke the news to Pip—and headed for the nearest bottle of Scotch. The alcohol didn't drown my sorrows—it only made them more pronounced. After going through one bottle, I swallowed some bennies so I'd be able to stay awake to drink another bottle. It wasn't one of my best nights.

In August, 1957, Joey Stevens traded in his black tux for Army khakis.

After eight weeks of basic training, I was assigned to Third Army Headquarters in Ft. McPherson, Georgia, as part of a Special Service entertainment unit. I was featured vocalist and master of ceremonies.

Leaving the glitter of the nightclub scene for the drudgery of basic training, guard duty, and KP was quite a letdown for me, but my attitude changed when, after basic, I became part of the Third Army Special Services Revue. I met a lot of tremendously talented fellows who turned out to be some of the greatest guys I have ever known. I didn't know then that within a few months, I was to experience the most important event of my life to that point: I was to meet my future wife, June.

I was first introduced to June, a gorgeous Southern blue-eyed blonde from Gastonia, North Carolina, by a mutual friend, Earl Chavell.

Earl had been telling June about me, urging her to go out with me. Whenever our Army entertaining troupe would be in Atlanta, we'd go to a Georgia Tech hangout known as the Wit's End. Well, Earl kept bugging her and after about three months she agreed to meet me there, but not as a date.

She told Earl she would rather drive over so she could leave if she wanted to. But the real reason was, I found out later, that she had a dinner date that evening with another guy. She went out with him and then, pretending she was ill, had him take her home. After he saw her to the door, she waited awhile and then drove over to the Wit's End where we were having a little jam session.

From the first moment I laid eyes on June, I immediately forgot all of the other girls I had ever seen before. If there's such a thing as love at first sight, it happened to me. And she later told me that she had the same reaction.

A few minutes after our initial introduction at a table, I went up to the bandstand in a half-dazed condition and sang four straight romantic ballads. Not once did my eyes leave June's. After my act, I went back to June's table, and we talked and we talked a while longer. Finally I asked her for a date the next day, but she had to turn me down because of a prior commitment to go boating. However, the next night, Monday, we went to Wit's End together, and from that point on, we began dating steadily, seeing only each other.

We had met on a Saturday and by that Monday—just two days later, mind you—we expressed our love for each other.

We were married July 19, 1959, by a justice of the peace in Atlanta. Neither of our parents attended the ceremony. In fact, I was so far away from Christianity that I didn't even feel it was important to discuss June's religion or religious convictions with her prior to our marriage. (As it turned out, she was the daughter of two wonderful Christian parents, Hazel and Raymond Braswell.)

Throughout my military service, which ended when I was honorably discharged in August, 1959, I continued to blow pot, take pills and drink heavily.

I did this even with a wonderful, devoted girl like June as a fiancée, and ultimately as my wife. The strange thing about Army life was that I used to get high on pot much more that I did when I was smoking marijuana during my civilian days.

A bunch of the Army musicians would sit around in the back of the bus and turn on. One day, we were so high we couldn't find the trombone player.

"I think he floated out the window," said the piano player, a fellow from Texas who always kept us rolling in the bus aisles with his humor.

After looking behind the seats and on the floor for the trombone player, we really started to worry about him.

"I told you he floated out the window," repeated the piano player. And by this time, most of us were convinced.

Finally, I found the missing musician.

He was sound asleep on top of the roof's luggage rack, arms around his trombone.

"Here he is," I told the boys, proud that I had made the discovery.

"Well, as long as he didn't float out the window, wake him up so we can split another one of his joints," said the piano player. The trombone case contained some stashed pot, but we couldn't wake our sleeping beauty. He was higher than high up there on that luggage rack, so we decided to let him rest while we hustled a couple of joints from the tenor sax man.

It seems strange, looking back on it all now—how we never considered the effects of smoking marijuana and drinking as heavily as we did. We laughed and joked and thought it was all a part of the game. Trouble is, we didn't realize that it's a game in which the players always lose. Sooner or later, the booze and the pot catch up with you. But no one could tell me that then. I knew it all—or at least I thought I did.

Well, that's the way it went throughout my stint in the Army.

It was a day-to-day kind of living, never worrying about tomorrow. Of course, I behaved myself a little better when I was around June, but my habits were gradually growing worse. Almost everyone could see that except me. Who knows, maybe even I could see it, but I wouldn't admit it, even to myself.

Upon being discharged from the Army, I returned to the 500 Club and tried to settle down as a contented married man. I was given back my old job as master of ceremonies. But once I began working the 500 and a few other night spots in the East, I noticed that married life had caused a big change in Joey Stevens. Maybe it was because I was more stable, but—whatever—I observed that at various cocktail parties and charity events at which I entertained, many important people, wealthy people, famous people, were all just going through the motions of life.

And for the first time in years, I thought back to the words of my father who used to preach from the Book of Mark: "For what shall it profit a man, if he shall gain the whole world, and lose his own soul?" (8:36).

During this period June and I went to see the motion picture *Ben-Hur.* It was the story of the crucifixion and resurrection of Jesus Christ.

Because we both had similar Christian backgrounds, the message of this film was the beginning of a turning point for us. From the time I had left the confines of my father's church, I had rebelled against everything good and holy.

Now after seeing *Ben-Hur* and being so moved by its message, I thought that perhaps I could accept Christ as my Lord, and dedicate my life to Him. Instead, I rebelled even more due to the evil power controlling me.

There's really no other way to describe it except to say that I was gripped by Satan. When I felt myself being moved by conscience, this other power seemed to overwhelm it, and, suddenly, I would hate the concept of Christianity even more than before. So there were these two great forces working on me simultaneously, but for the time being, the forces of evil were winning out. And I was helping the evil force by drinking even more—everything I could lay my hands on as often as I could. Besides this, I was taking pep pills such as Benzedrine, Dexamyl, Dexedrine and other types of drugs to keep me peppy and high enough to perform on stage.

This combination of booze and drugs left me with tremendous feelings of both self-elation and great remorse. While I was under the influence I would scorn and even curse my closest friends.

There was a story circulating about me that I was a regular Jekyll and Hyde. The story was accurate. At night in the club and in neighborhood joints that I frequented after the last show, I was a terror. I would start an argument at the slightest provocation. I would fall off the bar stool with sickening consistency.

By the next afternoon, however, after having a fair night's sleep and a couple of pep pills, I was smiling Joey Stevens once more, out doing the marketing with June or spending time dining in the many fine Atlantic City restaurants or jamming with the black musicians at Grace's Little Belmont or the Club Harlem during weekend matinees.

June and I would often double-date with friends on Sunday afternoons, we'd take leisure-time excursions to the Northside, and we'd all have a ball. After stopping at Grace's, the Timbuktu, the Harlem, Austin (Big C's) Johnson's Hi-Hat Bar, the Wonder Gardens, or Reggie Edghill's, we'd stop at Sapp's, or Jerry's, next to the Little Belmont, for spareribs. The "bones," as we called them, were finger-lickin' good and after we'd joke around with smiling Jerry for awhile and attempt to learn his special recipe for his hot sauce, we'd continue clubbing until I had to report to work.

I used to have a running commentary with Jerry about his sparerib sauce. A tall, husky black man, Jerry had a smile as broad as Liberace's and one of the loudest voices around.

"Hey, Joey," he'd scream in a piercing pitch whenever he'd spy me from behind the counter of his windowless wooden storefront.

"Man, do I have some bones for you today."

"Well how's the sauce, Jerry?" I'd counter. "You know, if the sauce isn't good, then the bones aren't good either."

"Don't worry about the sauce, Joey, my man," he'd say. "Look, I left that sauce outside in the back all week long just waiting for you."

Then, he'd wipe the grease from his hands on his soiled white apron, and in a stage whisper, confide to me, "You know, I've put my old stocking caps in that sauce, threw in some hot pepper, a squirt of tabasco and some leftover pickle juice, so you know it's gotta taste just right."

"Well, are you sure you put a used stocking cap in that sauce?" I'd say.

And big Jerry would roll his big brown eyes devilishly and answer, "Joey, baby, would I lie to you?"

"Of course not, Jerry, you wouldn't lie to me, so give me those bones because that sauce must be perfect."

Each time we'd go through our routine a small crowd would gather, trying to determine if we were for real, or if we were only playing around.

I never found out what Jerry really put in his sauce. All I know is that I enjoyed his spareribs as much as any choice filet I've ever eaten.

Reggie Edghill was known as the "Greatest Host on the Jersey Coast." His radio commercials and newspaper ads all carried this slogan, and Reggie did his best to live up to the reputation. He owned a string of clubs, a few smartly designed motels, a fleet of taxicabs and was a real sport when it came to spending.

On Sunday afternoons, I'd stop in at one of his Northside clubs and we'd have a few drinks. Then on Sunday evenings Reggie would drop by The Five for a chat, a sandwich, and a few more drinks.

Reggie saw what was happening to me.

"Joey," he'd say when he'd catch me at one of his matinees, "I don't want to lecture you, but we've been pals a long time and you have to cut this junk out. Drinking in the afternoon, drinking in the night, drinking in the morning, Joey, it's going to kill you."

"I know, Reggie," I'd reply. "But just cool it with me, baby. I'll be all right. Just let me swing to these sounds."

And I'd tap my foot, snap my fingers and lean my head back, grooving to the music in his club.

At night, Reggie would repeat the same admonition at the 500 Club. But, as usual, I wasn't buying.

On more than one occasion after a Sunday afternoon of this kind of frivolity, the male member of the couple with whom June and I were double-dating would stop by the club to see me, or take me home.

"Go away, I don't want to talk to you, you bug me," I would say nastily to my pal. Actually, it wasn't me talking, it was the booze. But my friends didn't know this and they were rightfully disturbed by my actions. When Skinny saw what was happening to me, he started to scold me.

"You've got to cut this out, Joey," Skinny would say. "You're killing yourself."

Skinny's brother, Willie, also tried to talk to me. I wasn't listening.

When Skinny and Willie directed the bartenders to limit the number of drinks I consumed, I merely slipped out of the 500 Club during breaks and drank somewhere else in the neighborhood.

I used to get so tore up from drinking and taking pills that Patsy Wallace, one of the bartenders at the 500 Club who acted like a guardian to me ever since my opening there, would have to pick me up bodily, carry me to his car and drive me home. Everyone except me, it seemed, knew I was heading downhill.

When I was high, I thought I was the greatest. When I came down, I was frightened to say hello to anybody for fear of what I might have said to them while under the influence of the booze and pills.

One morning, at about the crack of dawn, I was attempting to drive myself home in a borrowed car after hitting about six bars for nightcaps. I stopped for a red light in midtown Atlantic City and must have passed out at the wheel. The next thing I knew, a milkman making his early morning rounds was shaking me.

"What's a matter?" I slurred.

"You all right, buddy?" he inquired.

"Sure, I'm okay—beat it," I snarled.

"All right, wise guy," he answered. "I was only trying to help you out, but it's your funeral."

With that, the driver returned to his truck and I gunned my motor and shot away like a bullet—angry because the Good Samaritan had questioned my condition. I remember weaving down Atlantic Avenue at a high rate of speed, narrowly missing a pedestrian crossing the street.

When I entered Ventnor, which is a residential community just south of Atlantic City, I pulled over to the side of the street to buy an Atlantic City *Press* from a corner vending machine. I got out of the car, left the motor running, and the door on the driver's side wide open. I staggered to the vending machine and was all set to place the coins into it when I realized I didn't have any change.

In frustration and anger, I kicked the machine, unaware that a Ventnor police officer, attracted by my open auto door was observing my actions.

"Say fella, what are you doing there?" asked the policeman.

"Nothing officer, why? Are you going to arrest me?" I retorted sarcastically.

"You're Joey Stevens, aren't you?" he questioned.

"Yeh, I'm Joey Stevens. So what? What's that supposed to be —a big deal?" I said.

"It's not going to be any kind of deal if you don't calm down," the tolerant officer said.

Then he walked to my side, took some change out of his pocket, handed it to me, and said, "Here, Joey, you want a *Press?* Buy it. Then I'll park your car straight and you get into the police car and I'll drive you home."

He said it in such a compassionate manner that I started to weep. The sergeant placed his hand on my shoulder and with an understanding nod said, "Come on, Joey, I know how it is. . . ."

On the drive home, I found out that his name was Charley LaRe and that he was originally from Reading, and knew my family in York. He had seen me perform at the 500 Club on numerous occasions and said he had also enjoyed my performance during the several appearances I had made for the Ventnor Patrolmen's Benevolent Association Annual Benefit Show.

When he left me at my door, I thanked him with all my heart.

"Look, Joey," the sergeant said, "you don't have to thank me. But let me tell you something. Like I told you before, you'd better start calming down or else you're not going to be doing much singing anymore. You're going to wind up in the morgue."

And even though I was drunk, the thought sent a chill down my spine—but it didn't stop me from driving while I was drinking, because the next afternoon, shortly before I went to pick up my friend's car, I drank a half pint of gin.

One night I remember stepping on stage higher than the moon. I was singing at a banquet sponsored by a Negro Elks organization. I had been drinking all afternoon long, hadn't eaten any dinner, and had taken a few Dexies before I stumbled on stage.

Gazing out into the audience, I saw all those beautiful black faces and recalled my early days of gigging with black musicians. I started singing "Birth of the Blues" and when it came time for the chorus, I picked up my sax and started blowing. It was frantic. The crowd began handclapping in time with the song. The more they clapped, the more I blew. My eyes were shut tightly. Perspiration was streaming down my face. I was completely out of it. But the clapping continued. Then there were shouts of "Go, Joey, Go!"

After a solid thirty minutes of wailing, I laid down my horn and got into the end of the song. The Elks were screaming wildly. I went into the last line, hit a high note—and it happened. As I tilted my head back to get all I had into the finale of the number, the upper caps in my mouth flew out and landed next to a glass of whiskey being cradled by a woman at a ringside table.

The Elks roared with laughter, but I wasn't shook up at all. In fact, I was so cool about the whole scene, that all I did was bend down, lean over, pick up my caps, put them back in my mouth and finish "Birth of the Blues."

I was so high when the incident occurred that I couldn't remember it the next day, but most of Atlantic City had learned of the tale and it was something I never quite lived down.

Throughout this period, my precious wife, June, who was pregnant at the time, tried everything in her power to straighten me out. When I was high, I'd come home mornings in such bad shape that she'd plead with me to stop using pills and slow down my drinking "for our good," as she'd put it. But I wasn't listening to reason at that stage.

About two months before our baby was born, Bettyjane D'Amato threw a surprise baby shower for June. I had worked closely with Bettyjane for a few weeks before the shower, helping with the guest list and assisting her in the preparations. June had quite a few good friends in town, but many of the people invited to the shower were wives or girl friends of buddies of mine and people that I knew from around the club.

The shower was to take place in Skinny and Bettyjane's Ventnor home, and though I was busting to tell June about the secret, I didn't, even when I was high. At least I don't think I ever did. But if I did, June could have captured an Academy Award as best actress of the year—that's how stunned she was when she entered the D'Amato's home.

I drove her to the D'Amato's residence on the pretense that Skinny wanted to discuss some buiness with me and that Bettyjane wanted to visit with her. It was a Sunday afternoon, and as we climbed the brick stairs to the front porch, my heart was pounding. Actually, I was shaking like a leaf. I was nervous. I needed a drink. But before I had time to contemplate how I was going to sneak back into the car and take a swig from the bottle of gin hidden under the car's front seat, we were at the door.

I rang, Bettyjane shouted, "Come on in!" and I pushed open the front door to find about fifty women screaming, *"Surprise!"*

"Oh my gosh!" June stammered. Then her eyes filled with tears.

The living room was decorated with all types of baby-related ornaments, and in the center of the room were piled what seemed like hundreds of gifts. There were carriages, strollers, bassinettes, even a tricycle, baby clothes, and a playpen filled to the top with gift-wrapped packages of every shape, form, and description.

I scrammed as quickly as I entered, longing for the bottle under my seat, but just as I hit the bottom step, knowing that within fifteen minutes I'd be out swinging and drinking, a voice from within the house halted me in my tracks.

"Hold it, Joey, you can drive me to the club," Skinny called out.

When we arrived at the 500 Club, Skinny asked me to sit with him and have some coffee. Although I didn't have any plans to meet anyone, I was edgy because I wanted to get out to the Northside, see my Sunday afternoon crowd, eat some ribs at Jerry's, play some sax, and, of course, drink.

"What's the matter with you, Joey? Relax, will you? You're making me nervous wiggling around like that," Skinny said. "Everything's going to be great at the shower. You don't have to worry about that."

My mind wasn't even on the shower!

Then a lot of Skinny's pals stopped by the table, acting mysteriously about something. This made me even more fidgety. Finally, I couldn't take it any longer.

"Skinny, I've got to meet a couple of musicians who want me to go over some arrangements with them," I lied.

"Well, call them and tell them to meet you here," he said.

"Aw, I can't do that Skinny, they don't have a phone."

"Then just forget it," he said. "You've been stood up plenty before, now you stand these guys up and sit with us for awhile. You know, you hardly ever sit down and talk with me anymore, Joey."

Skinny had a sort of hurt look in his eyes. He had been so good to me, and here his wife was throwing a shower for a girl she didn't even know that well, and my desire for booze was causing me to become an ingrate to the very man I'd never want to harm in any way.

It wasn't easy, but I squirmed through a couple hours of conversation, drinking about six cups of black coffee.

I noticed that the fellows stopping by the table would only sit for a few moments, then depart abruptly. But I dismissed their unusual actions because I knew it was Sunday afternoon, and they had family chores they were probably going to perform.

I hadn't even considered picking June up from the shower because I knew I had to work at the club that night, and was certain she'd get a ride home with one of the girls. That's why, when Skinny and I were the last two remaining guys at the table, he shocked me by saying, "Let's go back and see how they're doing at the house."

Skinny wasn't the sort of man to participate in any type of women's activities, even though the activity might be occurring in his own home. But to atone for my uncooperative attitude earlier, I quickly agreed.

As we pulled up in front of the house, I saw that for some reason there were no lights on in the house. I thought this was weird, but didn't say anything to Skinny. Maybe they were showing home movies, or the tape of the Dean Martin-Jerry Lewis "Today Show." Sure, that was it, they were probably showing June the tape of that show.

Skinny knocked on the front door—which I also considered strange—but when the door was opened by June, I could see why the entire afternoon had had such a baffling air about it.

"*Surprise!*" the more than 100 guys and girls shouted to me. And looking at the faces around the room, I saw many of them were men that had a little earlier visited with Skinny and me at his table.

It was all crystal clear to me now.

Skinny and Bettyjane had arranged a two-part party. The first for June, the second for me. All of my pals, musicians from around the club, friends of Skinny's and the whole D'Amato family were on hand. And here I had tried to walk out on Skinny to get a few drinks. I felt like a heel.

But after a couple of drinks, I started to loosen up, and didn't feel so rotten. In fact, I started feeling great. This was like an army homecoming party for me and a welcoming party for June. In the afternoon, they had served tea sandwiches and champagne for the women, then when the men arrived, it was cocktails and dinner.

Everyone was in a tremendous frame of mind and there were toasts galore. Skinny warned me not to drink too much. "You've got to work later, you know," he said.

"Well, how 'bout if I start right now," I laughed.

I went over to a piano, sat down, and started belting out tune after tune. Honey Farley was there with her husband, State Senator Frank S. (Hap) Farley. The senator is one of the most powerful political leaders in the state. Whenever I sang for the Farleys, I always dedicated the song "Honey" to Honey Farley. That day, I sang it about six times. In fact, the whole crowd joined in.

The highlight of the party came when June cut a beautifully decorated, multi-tiered cake. In the middle of the cake the baker had designed a stork holding a baby. After I took June home and unloaded gift upon gift from the car, I rushed up to the club and worked three shows. I left about 3 A.M., started making the rounds of the after-dark spots, and by 5 o'clock was blind drunk. I was going to be a great father, I thought to myself disgustedly in my drunken haze. Really great. I was a disgrace.

On December 9, 1961, June Rebecca Boyer was born in Atlantic City Hospital.

The night before, I had driven June to the hospital between shows at the 500 Club. After I made certain she was being well cared for, I rushed back to the club for my next show. Hearing no word from the hospital after the last show, I decided to sleep on a couch in the office of the club which was just two blocks from the hospital. At noon the next day, I received a telephone call from Dr. Joseph D. Stella.

"Joey," Dr. Stella said, "you're the father of a baby girl and everything is in the right place."

8

Our home became a living hell for my wife and little girl.

THROUGHOUT MY TIME at the club I was in occasional contact with my parents. They, of course, were concerned about me, not so much about my nightclub career, but the fact I didn't know the Lord. I was missing the true meaning of life, they felt.

From this point on, after the birth of Junie in 1961, I developed an even greater dependence on drugs and booze. I began to realize that if I didn't take a pill and a drink that I would get nervous. It became increasingly hard to face people without these things in me. And instead of one or two drinks to get me going, I was having five or six and even drinking at home before I left for the club to do my first show.

It had reached the point where everytime someone said something about my drinking, I'd get mad.

"Leave me alone, man," I'd say. "It's my life."

I knew, however, that this drinking thing wasn't glamorous. I couldn't control it any longer and I finally began facing up to the grim fact that I had to drink to sing. To stand before an audience I had to have the stimulus of a pep pill and several drinks.

The effect of all this artificial stimulation on my personality was incredible. I would snap or growl at my best friends when I was under the influence, and when sober I would hate myself and feel ashamed. But this split personality wasn't only taking its toll on my friends. To an exaggerated degree, it was happening at home.

Our home became a living hell for my wife and little girl. I would come home high from the club and take out all my frustrations on them. As Labor Day weekend approached in 1964, the climax was beginning to unfold.

The Democratic National Convention had just been completed in Atlantic City and Eddie Fisher had just finished his stint at the 500 Club. Business, of course, had been excellent and I was putting in the hours. From 9 at night to 3 in the morning I was fine because the shows were popping. I was using the false energy of booze and pep pills to perform, but by the end of the evening or morning I would be completely zonked—not always falling-down drunk, but high, very high. I was either a bum or a king, and it got so bad that about a week before that Labor Day in 1964 I came home from an afternoon of drinking and hit my wife after I had started an argument with her. She bled around her eye and during the commotion, my daughter Junie fell out of the crib. The end had been reached. June told me she was going to have to leave for awhile.

"Go ahead—get out."

Then I told her I'd have her shot and thrown in the bay. Tears in her eyes, she replied, "You've said that before—you've threatened me before. But I'm going to leave this time. I have to—I'm afraid."

"Who leaves me?" I said. "I'll bust your head."

The fight took place a short time before I went to the club that night to do my show. I drank a couple shots of vodka and headed out. When I came home the next morning she really had split, taking Junie with her. I went into a rage. I stormed from room to room looking for her clothes. Some of them were gone, some were left behind.

When I finally began to understand what had happened, I couldn't cope with it. Knowing that she had truly left me was more than I could handle, mentally or emotionally. When she first cut out I felt sorry for myself in an egotistical way. How could she leave *me,* Joey Stevens? No one walked out on Joey Stevens—*he* walked out on other people. I split when I wanted to split, but nobody walked away from me. That's the way I saw it.

She has since told me that she didn't really want to leave, that she still loved me. But she had to because she feared for her own safety and that of Junie. She never knew what to expect when I was drunk—and neither did I. Sober, I was always good to her and loved her very much. But under the influence I was apt to do anything. Aware of that, she had to leave. It was her only choice.

I had lost more than a girl—I had lost my wife. That fact really hit me a few days later and I absolutely didn't know what I would do. I finally talked to her on the phone and she told me that she didn't know if she could ever come back—that it depended on my behavior.

June didn't flee for safety because of that one incident, although that was surely the straw that broke the camel's back. There were others, many others.

During the first summer when I brought her back to Atlantic City with me in 1960, things went fairly well. We were making a life out of it then even though I was doing shows every night and was drinking.

Night after night, coming home at sunrise, wasn't easy for her, but she thought I was making a career for myself and that things would get better. So she put up with it all those first months. And it might have lasted that way a great deal longer if I had been able to control myself.

After those first two years in Atlantic City, we went back to York for Christmas, to be with my family. And it was there, during those few days at home, that I realized what the other side of life was all about. I remember she told me on one of those days:

"Dave, [she never called me Joey] I just can't believe that you actually enjoy doing what you're doing." Ironically, she was right, but I wouldn't admit it.

One Thanksgiving we were sitting around with some friends watching television, when Billy Graham came on. Well, I started cussing him, and Christ, and everyone else. And that was one of the times she really expressed her anger at me.

"Just stop that," she said loudly.

So I gave it right back to her, snarling rudely, "I don't need you," I told her.

That was typical of what she put up with. I also told her on many occasions that it was she and our baby girl that were holding me back—slowing down my career.

June was always kind and sympathetic, however. She tried to understand what was happening to me and prayed that somehow things would be right again. She told me on one occasion, "I don't care if you work in a gas station as long as you're good to me and the baby. I just want you to be a good husband, that's all."

The fact that she put up with the cruel and evil way I treated her for so long is proof of how much she loved me.

I always had the ability to con her. I could sweet talk her and promise her great things. She wanted it that way so badly that she would believe me. But I always reverted back to the old ways of getting drunk and being nasty and mean to her.

My wife had ample reasons for leaving me long before she did. And she stayed convinced until the very end that I would change and become the kind of man she knew I was capable of being. Deep down inside, I did love her. But I guess I was afraid to let it show until it was too late. When she left, however, my life was shattered. That's when I stopped living, and began hitting the bottle as hard as it can be hit.

I was drinking so much, in fact, that one morning several weeks after she left, I woke up with blood in my mouth. Believe me, I was frightened. What had happened was that my gums had receded due to a pyorrhetic condition caused by malnutrition. I just wasn't eating.

People had noticed I was getting thin. Skinny had mentioned it to me, but it hadn't done any good. My dentist, Dr. Jack Slotoroff, gave me Vitamin C tablets and told me to drink a lot of orange juice. He also told me to lay off the booze for a while.

A few days later I called my parents and told them what had happened. And being the good parents they were, they came immediately to Atlantic City to see me.

My father, mother, and I went down to where June was staying in Margate, a suburb of Atlantic City, but June wouldn't let me in the room. So I took our little girl, Junie, and went out with my parents for the day. When we returned, my father left a note for June saying in effect that when he was sick, his wife took care of him. It went on to say that I was sick and needed June's help, though I had hurt her so deeply.

Even today June almost cries when she relates the story of that note. It didn't get us back together right away, but it did leave a tender feeling in her heart.

That first morning when my father arrived in Atlantic City I did something I really regret now. I had called because I was so ill, but he started talking about Jesus Christ, and I told him to shut up.

"Take your Jesus and get lost," I said.

But the dear man stood there with tears in his eyes and kept praying. The next day when he woke up he had to go back to York. He came to me and said, "It wasn't you talking last night. I love you and I'm not going to cease praying for you."

In spite of those terrible words of bravado to my father, the guilt that weighed me down was unbearable. It was shortly after this that I made the first attempt to take my own life. My sin had driven me to the breaking point. After existing on my inflated ego for so long, I found that I could no longer live on just that. The Benzedrine and alcohol had carried me along, but now none of these things provided what I *had to have* to live. Nothing was keeping me up.

One night I decided to walk into the ocean and end it all. I remembered all the nasty and cruel things I had done to people. I remembered what I had said to friends the night before—and I hated myself. How could I go back to them?

As it turned out, I didn't even have the courage to take my own life. I had started walking down Missouri Avenue toward the beach. It was my intention to just walk into the water and keep going until I drowned. But I couldn't do it. So I went home, changed clothes, and went out and got plastered instead.

I was scheduled to go to Boston that December in 1964, and then to Ft. Lauderdale, Florida. But just before the final arrangements were made, my father called and talked me into coming home for Christmas. It was my intention to go home for a couple of weeks, rest up, and then come back to Atlantic City and reopen at the 500 Club.

9

My father was mowing the lawn when God decided he had worked hard enough.

AS GOD'S WILL would have it, my life in Atlantic City had come to an end. Instead of returning to the 500 Club and picking up where I had left off, an event occurred that was to change the course of my life.

During that Christmas season of 1964 I stayed at home talking with my father and enjoying my mother's cooking. Oh, I did some occasional drinking at the local bars, and even got drunk a couple of times. But on the whole I was drying myself out and getting back some of my strength, both spiritually and physically.

My father and I discussed the Bible and the meaning of Christ, and it seemed to be doing some good. I began to get the feeling that I should get back with God, but the problem was that I didn't have the strength or the courage to give my life to Him.

One evening, after about two weeks in York, I stopped in for dinner at a place owned by an old friend I had met in Atlantic City. His name was Joseph (Jo-Jo) Sansome, and the place was Sansome's Colonial Inn in Marietta, Pennsylvania. Now, Mr. Sansome had heard I was having trouble with my marriage, and after talking things over for awhile, he asked me if I was interested in going into the restaurant business.

Well, I had always thought about having a piece of the action —I suppose every entertainer does. And this, coupled with the fact I was so broken up about June leaving—well, I thought it might give me a break in life. Perhaps being away from the club in Atlantic City—perhaps being in a new environment would get me straight again.

So I told Jo-Jo I'd be glad to have a piece of the place and work the inn. To top it off, he promised to build me an apartment adjacent to his beautiful home there in Marietta.

So I soon became the featured vocalist and part owner of the Colonial. Naturally, I was still drinking, not as much at first, but later I reverted to the old habit. And, indeed, it got worse, and as spring of 1965 began to roll around, many a night I sat with Mr. Sansome, me drinking V.O. and him drinking coffee.

Some days I would drink for hours on end—going through an entire evening completely zonked and right into the morning. Some mornings I would wake up so sick I was white—not sick at my stomach, but completely white from the alcohol saturation.

One Sunday I had nothing to do. I had been juicing all day, so I stopped at a club and for some reason decided to play clarinet with the band. Well, that's an instrument I hadn't played for years, but the audience said I was playing blues like they never heard. It was all coming out real because it was the only way I could express myself.

During the day I would sneak off to some saloons in the town of Marietta and listen to tunes, and just think about my family. One Sunday in May, 1965, I went over to my home. I was there in the evening and had been there for a few hours when my father came home from an evening service. We watched "Bonanza" on television (his favorite program), and before I left that night I did something I hadn't done in years. I kissed him.

"Dad," I said, "I'll see you."

And he answered as he always did, "I'll see you, boy. And don't forget, I'm praying for you."

It was the last time I saw him alive. That Thursday the bartender, Gabe, came to me while I was shaving, and said my mother had called to tell me that my father had just died. He was mowing the lawn when God decided he had worked hard enough.

My sister, Nancy, was the first one to get there, and I was the first boy home. When I got to my house I would have given all the money I ever had to know what to say to my mother. She had spent many sleepless nights because of me. She and my father would get on their knees and pray for me at night. My father would tell her, "Anna, trust God. God is going to save David, I know it." But when I got there that day she wound up comforting me.

"Son, I know how you loved him," she said, "but he's with Jesus, and you're not ready. I want you to be."

Well, I tried not to think of that. Some friends came over and brought a bottle of homemade wine. The whole board of the church came. We had to get in touch with everybody, naturally. When we finally got hold of Eugene in France, he declared firmly, "You tell the board of the church I'll be there in time to preach Sunday evening."

I'll never forget Mr. Sansome during this period. On Friday I had made a large bowl of spaghetti for everyone, and just about the time my mother was at her worst, in came Jo-Jo Sansome with an unbelievable assortment of imported foods. The odd thing was that no one could comfort her but him.

"Dear Jo-Jo," she said, and she had only met him once before!

He just grabbed her and said, "Mama." She just melted right there and became quiet.

By Saturday, my wife, June, had also arrived. As God would have it, she happened to call shortly after Gabe had told me about my father dying. So I told her what had happened, and she said she was coming to York for the funeral.

When it came time for the funeral I was standing alone beside the casket in the funeral home. Nobody was around at the time, and I looked down at my father. He was so peaceful with the smile of God on his face.

I said out loud to him there, "I wish I had had time to say I'm sorry. I'm sorry I called you 'square.' " (Many times as a teen-ager I had called him "Sam Square" right to his face.)

I walked away and saw my wife, June. She had a sincere look on her face as she said to me, "Dave, if you've ever done anything good in your life, why don't you do it now?"

I walked away from her without saying a word. But now I know that even then—after all the hell I had put her through—she was still trying to help me.

I went to church that night for services, and I'll never forget it because all the people Dad had known—his enemies as well as friends—were there. Even men like the neighbor that lived across the street (who thought my father was a nut because of his prophecies) came in respect. They didn't laugh or ridicule him then, because whether they agreed with him or not, they knew he was a man of God.

An English preacher who was a close friend of my father's, Dr. Ainsley Barnswell of the Baptist Church in Jackson, Michigan, gave the sermon which opened with this line:

"Absent with the body, present with the Lord."

This is indicative of the Christian faith. When a Christian dies, there is no time for worry or fear. The dead are with the Lord, and this was the belief that most of the people in the church held that day. To add on to that message and the telegrams, my mother walked to the piano at the end of the service. My brothers and sisters stood around the casket and I wound up standing there with them. We sang the old song, "Let's Keep on the Firing Line". It was our family theme song.

Let's keep on the firing line,
Let's advance our front for God.
Let's march with the greatest story to the world abroad
Let's go in Jesus' name unto every tribe and tongue,
Let's keep on the firing line till Jesus comes.

(Now I had had about ten shots of vodka at the bar around the corner and had taken four tranquilizers just to be able to stand this thing.)

When we got to the funeral home, my mother had complete control of herself. She was beautiful. "Thank you, Jesus. Praise God. He's with you now, and I'll see you both."

That's what she said at the grave, too.

That, however, was the faith I knew I didn't have. I could sense it there that day. I walked away from the graveyard convinced that I'd never see my father again. And I knew there was only one hope for me to ever see him and that was to find the Saviour that he preached about.

I returned to the parsonage with my family where we gathered around and sang all the songs we had sung as a family group so many years before.

June went back to Atlantic City. She had to—because I really hadn't changed. She knew and I knew that the same thing might happen again. By the following Friday, I was back in Jo-Jo's belting the songs, downing the booze, and growing lonelier and lonelier.

Throughout the period following my father's death, one verse kept coming to mind:

"For what shall it profit a man if he shall gain the whole world and lose his soul?" It kept going through my mind to the point I couldn't sleep at night, even with all the alcohol I was drinking and the pills I was taking.

At the inn when I sang "Who Can I Turn To?" or "The Party's Over" or "The Thrill is Gone" or "I'll Never Smile Again," I knew what I was singing about. Those songs were my life then. They reflected my entire existence. The crowd dug it because it was coming from the heart and soul, but what was it doing to me? There was no peace. And every night I'd lay in that bed and wish I could say:

"Reverend, Reverend, I'm sorry." But it was too late. And I'd have given anything I ever had or would ever have just to have my wife and little girl back. Jo-Jo could sense this, and he was understanding, but at the same time there was nothing anybody could do for me.

August rolled around that 1965. By this time the sin that had controlled my life since I was a teen-ager had run its course. Even though for weeks and months I had tried to be a better man, I couldn't. I had to depend completely on the use of alcohol and drugs to do my gig. Worse than that, there weren't enough drugs and alcohol to take away the guilt. I've talked to psychiatrists today who say that if they could rid people of their guilty feelings, 90 percent of the people who are in asylums wouldn't be there. Of course, there is a way to do that. A belief in God's forgiveness and devotion to Him is the greatest psychotherapy going, but I wasn't quite ready to accept that yet.

10

*I realized I could live, but it would have to be for God
—not Joey Stevens.*

ON SATURDAY NIGHT in York, August 29, 1965, I was singing all the old songs and carrying on in my usual asinine way. And the song titles were so reflective of my life:

"Only the Lonely", "Set 'em up Joe", "Happiness Just is a Thing Called Joe"—all the grabbers—the songs that ring of sadness and nostalgia.

We wrapped it up late that Sunday morning, and after a few more drinks and a couple of pills, I went to bed. But I didn't sleep more than three or four hours. I awoke later on Sunday morning remembering that I couldn't get a drink in Pennsylvania except in private clubs. But it was early, and even the American Legion was closed.

I waited around and later called my buddy, Gabe, and we ended up hitting some private clubs around town. Finally, at about eleven that evening we wound up in a private club in Marietta.

Now throughout this day, my guilt and depression had been greater than it ever had been. I don't exactly know why, but on that day it was. I thought about the way I treated my father, and had never been able to tell him I was sorry.

I kept thinking about how badly I had treated June and Junie. The guilt on my conscience became so great that I couldn't cope with it. If I had been given millions of dollars and a hit record at that moment it wouldn't have made any difference.

And ironically, my predicament wasn't really unique. Many entertainers are in the same boat. They're happy and laughing on stage and in crowds, but back in the dressing rooms many of them are miserable. Many of them, like me, had no deeper purpose to their lives. I knew it. And I kept thinking about my father's messages and what he tried to tell me. As usual, that one line kept coming back to me:

"What shall it profit a man . . . ?"

I had enjoyed all the pleasures of life. The girls, the booze, the wild times, the success of show business. Yet here I was lonely, disgusted, and busted because of selfishness. My guilt was so great I didn't want to live. I was at a point where I had to take drugs and booze in order to be able to do the things that were no longer fun. What were kicks for me at eighteen had become bad habits. I was hooked on them. And I had completely reversed. I wanted to be clean, and I wanted my wife instead of being an adulterer. I didn't want to be a swinger; I didn't want to be famous. I just wanted to be a family man. I wanted to stop drinking, but I couldn't. I didn't have the strength. My kidneys were nearly shot. The pain was so bad sometimes that I nearly jumped off the bar stool. So a sense of hopelessness really gripped me that Sunday night even more than it had before. I didn't think I would ever see my wife and child again.

Throughout that summer, whenever I got drunk I would talk about religion—about wanting to get back with God. Gabe got fed up with it after awhile.

"The only time you talk this way is when you're drunk," he'd say to me—and he was right.

That Sunday night I said the same thing. But I added something:

"You won't see me again, Gabe."

With that, I had my last double shot of bourbon, swallowed a couple of pills and stumbled out the door.

"You'll be all right in the morning, Joey," Gabe told me. He was right, of course, but for reasons he couldn't have known then.

As I walked out of the club I knew I was going to commit suicide. It was the end of the line for Joey Stevens. I crossed the street and began walking to the railroad tracks a few blocks away, where I was going to throw myself on the rails and wait for a train to crush me. As I walked I cried and I prayed. I asked God to give me the strength to live even as I headed for what I thought would be my death. I passed by an old church as I staggered down the street and fell on the steps leaning back against the stone pillars. I literally beat my head against that church crying.

"God let me live for you—give me the strength—somehow."

I'm not sure exactly what happened at this point. All I remember is that a feeling came over me—an awareness of God's love for all men, even those such as me who cursed His name. And for a moment there was a feeling of peace and security. I realized that I could live, but it would have to be for God, not myself—not Joey Stevens. The meaning in my life would have to be translated in terms of what God wanted—not what I, Dave Boyer, wanted.

I sat there for a few minutes as the Spirit of Christ began filling my heart. This was the conversion my father and mother had always prayed for. This was the moment of truth when the power of righteousness overcame the power of evil. It was as if I had been born again, given new hope and a new way. At that moment Joey Stevens died. He became nothing more than a memory of times past—of horrible sin and an evil life. In this place sat a tear-faced Dave Boyer, the man who was born for something more meaningful than a bust-out song and a bottle of booze.

I got up slowly from the steps of that old church, sober as a judge. And I knew precisely what I had to do.

Almost running to a nearby phone booth, I called my brother,

Gene, who was at home in York at the time, and told him that I wanted to find Christ and accept Him into my heart.

I knew I had to come over to Christ and I wanted Gene to be my witness. I wished then that my father had still been alive—that he could have been my witness. But this was the second best thing, and I knew that Dad was with me in spirit. It would have pleased him mightily to know that his prayers had finally been answered, that the God of life and hope had once again touched one of His own creations in a very personal way.

"Wait right there, boy," Gene said when I told him.

And he came in a few minutes. I learned later that he called Mother and said, "Put the coffee on, Dave's coming home."

When I was thirteen, Gene told me in the living room one day; "You don't have enough guts to live for God." Now, there he was at 1 A.M. driving me back to York Gospel Center, my dad's church. We opened it up and I raced down the aisle to the old wooden tabernacle-type altar. Believe me, I literally *ran* to that old altar and told God I was giving my life to Him. But it had to be more than just to quit drinking and popping pills. Christianity is more than just what you don't do. It's what you do with your will.

You must completely give your will to that of God. And this is what happened on the night of August 29, 1965, in my father's church.

Gene asked me in words loud and clear:

"Dave, do you know you're a sinner?" And I said *yes.*

"Do you believe God loved you enough to forgive you of sin?" Again, I said *yes.*

"Do you believe He still loves you even though you beat your wife and cursed Dad?" Again, I said *yes.*

"Are you going to give Christ whatever you have?" *Yes,* was the answer.

"Do you believe that the strength that let Jesus Christ rise from the grave will come into your life and take away the desire for drink and drugs?"

"Yes," I replied.

And then it happened. In that church it happened. And I am alive today as a living testament to the fact that God came into my life.

I stood to my feet a new man.

"Praise God," Gene said.

And we were brothers united in the spirit of Christ. I walked out of the church and up the steps of the parsonage and my mother didn't have to hear a word from me.

She looked at me and said, "David, your countenance has changed. Jesus is in your heart."

I knew what I had to do the next day. It couldn't wait. I had to go to my partner and friend, Jo-Jo Sansome, and tell him I was through. And that wasn't the easiest thing to do because he had been good to me.

Gene drove me over to the inn, remaining in the car while I went to the door. He told me later he was praying for me all the while he waited.

Mr. Sansome was out front pruning his evergreen trees.

"Joey, baby," he called out.

With a straight face, I said, "Jo-Jo—I gotta tell you something. Right up the street I met Christ last night." And I went on to tell him the whole story.

"What I'm saying, Jo-Jo, is that I've got to quit. Nothing against you—I love you. You've been a great friend, almost like a father to me. I don't know what I'm going to do, but whatever it is I'm going to do it for the Lord."

He said he had to think about it. He went inside, came back out, and we got into his car and began driving around town.

First of all he said I was hung up because of my wife. Then he said it was in my mind—that I had been drinking.

"I'm building you a new apartment, and you got a piece of the action at the inn," he said.

"It's not a question of what I have a piece of, Jo-Jo," I said. "It's just that I want out. I want to live for the Lord and whatever He wants me to do."

He thought for a moment, and then said very quietly and seriously, "If you do this, Joey, you can't go around living the way you do now."

We drove back to the house, shook hands and parted friends. So I went back home with my brother, Gene, and there I was. I had spent all the money I ever made, so I didn't know what I was going to do.

On Tuesday, June called the restaurant and asked for me. Gabe told her, however, that I had gone home.

"Joey gets religious when he gets drunk now, so he's over home."

She called York, and I told her on the phone a line I'll never forget.

"June, last night I met Christ as my Saviour."

There was a few moments of silence and almost in a tearful voice, June said, "I believe you! I believe you!"

We talked for a while and she was very excited. She knew it was for real then, and she told me later she just prayed that nothing would happen to make me lose that faith.

The next day, Wednesday, Gene told me he really believed that I had found God and that he wanted me to sing at a prayer meeting.

At the church that night I asked my mother what I should sing. She showed me a *Favorites* book and said, "That's between you and God."

The song that came to me right off was "No one Ever Cared For Me Like Jesus."

I looked at the pulpit and remembered that my father had preached there. I remembered that Dr. Billy Graham had preached there. I remembered all those men who had stood in that pulpit— Godly men who had given themselves to the Lord and I was aware that in just a moment I was going to stand at that same place.

And believe me, I looked ahead and said, "God, I'm not worthy of this. I'm just not worthy."

But the great thing about God's love for us is that men like me, men who have sinned and spat upon Him, are still in His eyes. He looks back and says "Father, forgive them—they know not what they do."

When I was aware of this, of what He had done for me, I was overwhelmed. So when I walked to the pulpit the words and the music of the song came out.

> I would love to tell you what I think of Jesus,
> Since I found in Him a friend so good and true.
> I would tell you how he changed my life completely
> He did something that no other friend could do.
>
> All my life was full of sin when Jesus found me,
> All my life was full of misery and wrong.
> Jesus placed His strong and loving arms around me
> And led me in the way I ought to go.

Nowadays I sing songs like this to kids in coffee houses—old hymns—and they melt down through the drugs and immorality. Kids realize this is not some far-out, rolling-on-the-floor type of reaction. This is the reality of man meeting God. This is what happened in that prayer in the York Gospel Center that night.

I lived in my mother's home at that time. Her marvelous Christ-like strength and support carried me through some very difficult days as I struggled to get on my feet—both as a newborn Christian and as a man. With quiet understanding and sympathy my mother knew what I was going through. When I came home at night I would walk those steps asking, *God, when are you going to bring June home?*

But I couldn't come to Christ just to get my wife back; I had to come to Jesus for Himself. He is a jealous God and He says He is. I had to dedicate not only my will, but everything. I had to love Him enough to say, "If You don't want me to sing, I still love You. Whatever it is, even if June doesn't come home, I'm still going to love You."

Then everything began to fall in place. I made my first record album in June of 1966. I was singing around various churches when two men, Harold Dubbs and Herb Lippy of Hanover, Pennsylvania, got interested in my singing and invested enough money to record my first album. It was produced at Capitol Customs under the Reverence Label of Baltimore, Maryland.

Since that time, with my friends Dr. Edwin Pierpoint and Dick Thoman, we have released four albums and the company has grown quickly. (Dick is vice-president of the firm, and our accountant. Without his help there just wouldn't be a record company, and the Evangelistic Crusade would not be possible.)

During 1965, I got a few breaks with other churches. I was singing with Gerry, my brother, and his wife, Eleanor.

By January I had completed a tour of Minneapolis booked by my brother, Dan, and came home to the biggest thrill of my life. I welcomed back for good my wife, June, and daughter, Junie.

Several months later we moved into an apartment. From there we began making more albums. My ministry to teen-agers began growing to a fantastic scope that now we sometimes speak to 30,000 to 40,000 kids a week in high-school assemblies; but I don't believe in doing just big services. I think it's as important to talk to five as it is to 5,000.

I had the privilege of being selected by the National Evangelical Film Foundation as the Most Outstanding Male Vocalist for three years, and was also awarded the best overall record of the year for our 1968 *New World* album.

Because of Christ, our family and home are filled with God's love. Our nine-year-old daughter Junie accepted Christ as Lord in her seventh year. My wife also walks close with Christ having found Him when she was twelve.

It's really a joy to see how God can give strength to our home, especially when I am away so much. Early in 1970 we lost a son who was stillborn. Even at this tragic time, June insisted that I go on to Michigan for meetings as planned, instead of staying home with her. "God's work is more important," she declared.

June is Secretary-Treasurer of Reverence Records and of our Evangelistic Crusade. Just to make it a complete family affair, Junie is practicing with me now. God has really blessed her with talent.

What a joy to serve the King of kings as a family! This life, even with all its trials, is a victorious one when lived by His power.

I know that my success at this point is due to the presence of the Holy Spirit of God in my life, whether I am singing in a church, on a street corner, or talking to a troubled kid on the telephone.

Whatever situation God puts me in, I feel it is my duty to let Him get through. By that I mean, it is not my reward now to hear how great I am. It is, instead, to know that people have found peace and contentment by accepting a life in Christ.

To do that I can't stand in the way of Lord. It is to His honor and glory that I am Dave Boyer again—not Joey Stevens.

11

Gigging for God

In 1969, I was in a coffee house on the Southside of Chicago which brought back memories of my days spent there on my record promotion tour in 1954. At that time I was told I was destined for stardom. Now I was back in Chicago, playing a different game, not the least bit concerned about stardom, but only about spreading the word of Christ.

As I began to work in the coffeehouse, four guys in long hair and leather jackets began screaming and attempting to make trouble.

I used an old nightclub tactic for putting down hecklers. I told them to shut up or get out, and I did it in such a way that they became quiet. So I did the contemporary religious songs that I've done on my albums and gave my story, warning them of the dangers of drugs and the overuse of alcohol. By the time I had finished, some of the boys actually had tears in their eyes— not for me, but from the melting power of the Holy Spirit of God.

As soon as I finished I walked right to their table. There were twelve there (with their girls), and I sat down and began to talk.

"What do you want?" I questioned them. "Ask me. I don't promise an answer, but I'm here to help."

One boy said, "Dave, how can you get off of drugs once you're on them?" He tried to make it sound as if he were referring to another person, but I knew he was asking it for himself.

Another boy said that all the preachers he had known made God seem like He's on a pedestal, somewhere out there where they can't get to Him.

"To me," he said, "God should be your buddy."

"God's the greatest buddy anybody could have," I replied. "Although He's a universal God, He's as personal and as close as you want Him to be. All you have to do is believe that—have that faith."

Before I left the coffee house, one the boys named Chris, said, "Dave, we've got something we want to give you."

I held out my hand and to my astonishment he placed some pot in it.

I looked around at first. I didn't want to be a patsy for anybody, but I felt free and took it.

The kid was crying a little and he said, "I trust God. I don't need this."

I got outside and looked in my hands and then I really started to weep. I drove down the street and threw it out of the car. The powerful ending to this little story is that more than a year later, I received a letter from one of the two boys saying he had not only given up pot, but had gone to the local Youth for Christ representative and said he wanted to accept Christ. The letter said, in part:

Hi Dave,

I don't know if you remember me, but when you were in Chicago about six months ago you sang at Bogan's Coffee House, and afterwards you talked with two guys, Danny (in the suede jacket with fringe) and me (Chris). I also gave you something to get rid of for me. Now that you know exactly who's writing to you, I want to say thanks *a lot*. You really gave me a lot of answers to a lot of my problems. After you left that night, I talked with Dave Rinbald and Ron Huchcraft and told them I wanted to know more. Since then I have accepted Christ and have been walking around *high* ever since. I was really shocked by how beautiful this kind of high can be. And when you told me *He* helped you love a lot more people, you weren't kidding. I stopped hating my dad and other people who cared for me.

I thank Jesus for getting me to meet you and the rest of the guys in YFC [Youth for Christ.] I've even been able to help a couple of people. I had a friend that used to steal cars all the time, and he got caught many times, but one time just before I got to him he got caught red-handed. He met Christ through me and he's really changed.

Take it easy,

Chris Z. (a Christian)

Again, in Chicago about a year ago, a kid got so turned on he wanted to disrupt the whole conference. Three hundred people came into the school to hear me that day, and when I was answering questions he would ridicule everything I said.

"Shut up, man," I told him. "If you don't want to listen, get out. I came a long way to talk to these kids. A lot of kids like you used to laugh; now they're in the gutter, addicted to heroin."

After the conference had ended, he came up to me and said,

"Mr. Boyer, I'm sorry for the way I acted. This was some message."

Today this boy is like the missionary of the high school. The principal wrote the Youth for Christ director and said, "I don't know what's happened, but this change is fantastic."

I really don't preach during these conferences. I sing, play my horn and tell my story.

I was in another high school in Chicago which had been having terrible racial problems. It was so bad, in fact, that I was taken to the principal's office by armed guard.

The principal told me that he wasn't sure anyone would show up for the assembly at which I was scheduled to sing and talk.

"It's the last period of the day, and they don't have to come if they don't want to. We have tough militants here of both colors. We'll promise you'll be safe, however, but that's about all," he said.

Now the conference was going to be held in the gymnasium, which is a hard place to work in the first place. If a kid even so much as drops something, it rings out all over the house.

At these conferences, I set up my tape recorder which has the same score and background as my records, but without my voice. In that way, I don't have to mouth the songs, but can actually sing them live, and the audience gets the same sound as the record itself.

As I finished my first song, a black kid started yelling, sarcastically "Get your sax and play some jazz, honky. Blow your horn, blow your sax, Whitey."

Finally I had about all I could take and said: "Shut up or leave, man. I got a song to sing. I've faced wise guys all my life, so just get out if you don't like what's happening here."

He got quiet after he saw the rest of the students digging me. I sang "I Believe," and they were with me. And for the last song I did an uptempo version of the old Negro spiritual, "Just a Closer Walk With Thee." Before I knew it they were singing along, clapping their hands and weaving back and forth, black and white alike.

When I walked out of there I didn't get a standing ovation, but I received polite applause.

Now, I want you to know that this is not my glory, because all I did was get out of the way of the Lord.

The Bible says, "And I, if I be lifted up . . . will draw all men unto me" (John 12:32).

So this is the thing. If I go right now to the 500 Club and sing, I might get a fine ovation.

"Nice job, Joey," somebody might say.

But when I sing now I don't want people to remember Joey Stevens. That is why I don't get involved even with a love song. I would have to have a love thought or a physical thought to sing a love song and sing it well.

I sing to make people aware of a great eternity with God. And the only way they'll remember Him is if I'm out of the way. More than Joey Stevens or Dave Boyer, they've got to see God in what I do. That's it—or I've got nothing else to live for.

". . . seek ye first the kingdom of God . . . and all these things shall be added unto you" (Matthew 6:33).

That's His promise. I believe it.